T0193092

Nuts to Butts

Anecdotes from a Career in the US Navy

R. W. Bishop, USN (Ret)

iUniverse, Inc.
Bloomington

Nuts to Butts
Anecdotes from a Career in the US Navy

iUniverse books may be ordered through booksellers or by contacting:

iUniverse
1663 Liberty Drive
Bloomington, IN 47403
www.iuniverse.com
1-800-Authors (1-800-288-4677)

ISBN: 978-1-4759-0590-8 (sc)
ISBN: 978-1-4759-0589-2 (hc)
ISBN: 978-1-4759-0588-5 (ebk)

Library of Congress Control Number: 2012905566

Printed in the United States of America

iUniverse rev. date: 04/23/2012

Contents

For My World War II
Heroes

My Father
John W. Bishop, USN (SS)

My Uncles
Kenneth L. Bishop, USN
Ralph D. Curts, USN
James J. Perlongo, USA (POW)

My Father-in-Law
Alfred W. Mooney, USA

Acknowledgments

I would like to thank my wife, Donna, for her endless hours of proofing this manuscript. She also kept me fairly straight on punctuation—no small task, to say the least. The same thing concerning proofing could be said about both my sons, Seth and Steven, and my sister-in-law, Denise Lanter. I also want to thank Linda Mueller, who was always so supportive when we discussed this project, and Bonnie Marston for her invaluable assistance. Others I would like to thank include Mary Harkless and Leonard Southerland, former coworkers who gave me constant encouragement, and Ernest G. Zumbrunnen, author of *The Kid Was a Hustler* (2010, iUniverse). His help and sage advice got me off the launching pad. I also give thanks to all those who served in the navy with me over the years and especially those whom I supervised. You know who you are, and you kept my chestnuts out of the fire a million times. I hope you all look back on our association with fond memories. I do.

Finally, I would like to thank those of you out there whose actions have now become fodder for my literary cannon. Without you, this book would not have been possible. I am still thinking. Maybe there is a volume two in my memory bank.

Introduction

The first thing to remember when reading this work is that the reflections or recollections contained herein are mine and only mine. Just as witnesses to an accident are likely to disagree on some of the facts, so too would some of my former shipmates, I am sure, not agree on the way I present it. Everyone sees every situation differently than those around them when it is happening. By the time I got around to writing this book I was twenty years and forty pounds past active duty. Now in my sixties, I see things with a little more humor and clarity, I hope, than I did when my navy career depended upon getting the record right. I am by no means senile but consider myself a bit wiser and maybe a little clouded on the chain of events. With the exception of a few well-known personalities of national note, I have tried my best to keep actual names out of this endeavor. Unfortunately, that is a lot easier to say than to do. When necessary, some names have been changed. If I slip and a name gets into the final product, please forgive me. I have burned a lot of midnight oil on this project. In an effort to keep actual identities secret I have also kept the names of commands and ships to a minimum. I was afraid that to identify the action and the command would be to identify the individual concerned. Some of them might not mind so much, but I am sure that some may be embarrassed, even though that is furthest from my intent.

This work is not intended to be a tell-all wherein I spill the beans on the US Navy, any of my shipmates, or myself. The views expressed are mine and only mine. The incidents presented in this book are explained as I remember them. I present them in no particular order except I start at the beginning of my career. My years in the navy were peppered with some unfortunate events that will always stay with me. I deal with them in my own way, and this is not the venue in which to discuss them. Today I can laugh at some of the things I encountered during my military career. But I only laugh at some of them. I hope you can laugh with me.

What is with the name of the book? The title, *Nuts to Butts*, refers to one of the first phrases I learned while in basic training in 1969. A second phrase I learned in boot camp was the old hurry-up-and-wait adage. Recruit companies are always in a hurry to get where they are going so they are not late and do not miss whatever is planned for them. Usually, when they arrive at their destination, the company prior to them has not left yet. Soon the company scheduled after them is arriving, and the whole area gets pretty crowded. Company Commanders start tightening up the lines of recruits. You hear a lot of, "Closer! Closer! Get closer!" and then, finally, you hear, "Put your nuts against their butts!" This continued the whole visit because there was never enough room. So, those two phrases became words to live by for recruits.

As I think back over the years, the phrase "nuts to butts" is pretty indicative of many operations and evolutions I was privy to. You are always being told to hurry up, and you end up waiting for someone else to finish his part. When you are waiting, leaders are constantly telling you to get closer to the job and get ready to jump in there. Nuts to butts, so to speak. After all those years I have developed a habit that is hard to break. Whenever I am in a line somewhere I try to get as close as I can to the person in front of me. That served me well in the navy, but when you are in line at Target, Wal-Mart, or other similar store, it is not really appreciated. It still bothers me if there is a gap in a line because someone is not paying attention or moving up when they should.

I so want to scream, "Nuts to butts, up there!"

R. W. Bishop

Gladstone, Oregon

September 8, 2011

Chapter 1

"We're not in Kansas anymore."

Oath of Enlistment

I, _____, do solemnly swear (or affirm) that I will support and defend the Constitution of the United States against all enemies, foreign and domestic; that I will bear true faith and allegiance to the same; and that I will obey the orders of the President of the United States and the orders of the officers appointed over me, according to regulations and the Uniform Code of Military Justice. So help me God. (Military.com, 2011)

My navy career really began on Thursday, August 7, 1969. That is the date my mother drove me the sixty-some miles from Pinckney, Michigan, to Fort Wayne in Detroit to get my enlistment physical and sign even more papers. We had to be at the fort by five in the morning. We had to get up and out of the house by zero dark thirty to make the deadline, which I now know to be "oh five hundred hours." I had no idea what to expect and did not want to be late and piss them off on the very first day. After all, I had copies of my official orders in my possession. The orders I had were signed by representatives of the president of the United States. Richard M. Nixon held that position that summer. Surely these were nothing to sneeze at. National defense was probably at stake, and if I was late I would miss the boat. Mom had the situation under control, and I got there with time to spare. Was she trying to get rid of me? She parked the car along the curb a short distance from the entry point that I was supposed to use, and I got out. I showed my official orders to the Military Policeman, the MP, at the gate and was admitted onto US government property for the first time.

As I reflect back on the day of my physical, I remember that Fort Wayne was not in the most secure area of Detroit. While I was jumping through hoops set up by the examining board, which included bending over and spreading my cheeks (did I really see them use a flashlight), my mother had the unenviable task of waiting in her car on the street all by herself. She was the only person waiting along the curb. Throughout the day my mind kept returning to wondering about her safety. My day at the fort was going to be from six to eight hours. She would spend that entire time reading a book in the car, and in the middle of an August heat wave. Though I did not know it at the time, my worries were taken care of when the MP at the gate walked over to our car and invited her to park next to the gate house in the Official Vehicle spot. He told her he would feel more comfortable with her nearer him than down the street where he could not keep a good eye out for her. He must have left his post to do that. I do not know who that guy was, or whether he was a marine or a soldier. As I made it through my career I built a list in my mind of people who have done something that has helped me in some way without reward. I have silently thanked them from the bottom of my heart and on too numerous of occasions for being there and doing what they did without asking for a favor in return. That unknown MP on the gate at Fort Wayne, Detroit, was the first person on my "Thank God for Being There" list. There would be more.

The day of my examination was the first glimpse I had that I was not in Kansas anymore, or in my case Pinckney, Michigan. I had been in the high school locker room plenty of times and had seen and showered with naked guys before. This was a different scene, however. I had never seen so many different races, ethnicities, and international heritages or backgrounds. This was also the day I learned the painful truth, that I was not as well-endowed as I had always thought. Toto, we were definitely not in Kansas, anymore. During the day I acted in my very best Silent Cal mode, referring to President Calvin Coolidge (1923–29). My interaction with the masses around me was limited by some advice given to me by a friend of my older brother who had served in the navy. His advice was to keep your mouth shut, pay attention to people around you, and do not trust anyone until you know them well enough, and then still be very cautious. That was good advice that I have used many times in my life since then, and it has never let me down.

Another learning experience happened when we were taken to the chow hall to eat lunch or chow down, slop grits, fill the old pie hole, or any number of other euphemisms. Remember that it was a hot day outside. It was pretty hot inside the chow hall too. Large fans with blades that had to be at least three feet across were located strategically around all the tables in the hall. These fans were just blowing up a storm while we were trying to eat what I think were fish patties. Only one per person, please. The lesson I speak of came after I sat at my assigned seat. I was trying to keep my napkin from flying off the table when, I swear this to be true, my fish patty actually flipped over on my tray. Luckily it stayed on the tray, although I would have probably eaten it anywhere it landed. The lesson here was be prepared for anything in a military chow hall. That does not actually apply to air force dining facilities. That is right; I did not call it a chow hall. Air force dining facilities are in a league of their own. If you ever get the opportunity to dine at one, do not pass it up.

In the future I would be reminded of this fish patty incident on those occasions when the ship served meals on the helicopter landing deck (helo deck). They called it a steel beach picnic. It was usually held on a Sunday afternoon. Crew members could wear pretty much what they wanted, for instance, cutoffs and T-shirts. Many guys brought up their boom boxes for music. Some played basketball or tossed a ball, among other activities. The ship's cooks grilled burgers and dogs along with the appropriate condiments. It all sounds like fun, and it was a nice gesture by the ship to try and bring the beach party feel to midocean. However, it is very hard to eat outside with what seemed like a 40-knot wind across the deck. The local sea life got its fair share of potato chips on these days. Paper plates, plastic utensils, napkins, and lettuce never had a chance. Like the fish patty in the chow hall, everything loose blew over the side.

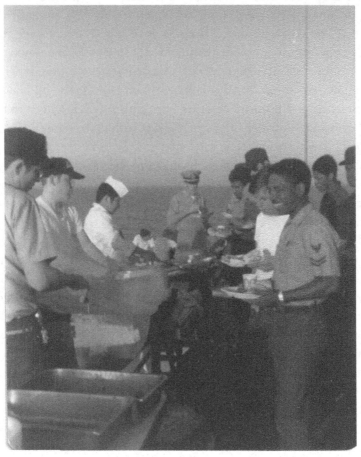

Steel beach picnic on USS *LaSalle*, 1976.

At some point during the day we were given hearing tests. These tests are probably fairly standard around the nation. Eight to ten people are placed in a big soundproof box with four to five stations on each side. Everybody in the box sits at a station and dons a headset. Various tones are fed to each person through the earphones, and they react as directed when the sound starts and stops. When you first hear a tone you push a handheld button and hold it until the sound disappears, and then you let up on the button, signaling an end to that cycle. The tones continue to come and go in each ear until all testing tones are done. When the hearing test is complete you are removed from the box, and another group goes in. It is all done with military precision.

Once you are out of the box the corpsman does a cursory look at the computer card that represents your hearing test graph, and if it looks good he places it in your file, hands the file to you, and off you go to the next physical indignity. If there are any problems with the card or if you appear to have a hearing deficiency, then you are returned to the box for a retest using the same card with a different color ink to make the second graph. The guy next to me had such a problem. He had been through the test before me, with me, and then was going after me. There would be at least three different colors of graphs on his card. After he was in the booth for the third time and we moved to the next part of the physical, I thought I would not see him again.

I could not have been more wrong, however. Since some tests are time sensitive, he would pop in and out of our group in between hearing tests. Every time I saw him again he had additional colors on his card. At the time I figured he was just stupid, and it was cracking me up. But having spent many years not in Kansas anymore, I realize that he may have been trying to fail the physical because he had been drafted. Being from Pinckney, I was naive enough to think we were all there voluntarily. But, Vietnam was going hot and heavy at that time, and draftees would most likely go to the Southeast Asian paradise. I look back from a present-day vantage point, and I do not blame him.

It turned out to be an interesting day, all-in-all. I had been physically examined twenty-six ways from Sunday. I now knew what it was like standing naked in a roomful of men from all walks of life and morals. Certainly there were men with criminal pasts. Most people have heard stories of judges giving an option at sentencing of military service or jail. It seemed apparent to me that a few of the guys in line were there because they opted out of a jail lifestyle. A number of them had what I thought were gang tattoos. Some congregated in small groups, talking among themselves and cautiously watching the others around them. If there had been a clique that I fit into, I would have joined them in a heartbeat.

Personal hygiene was not at the top of the things-to-do list for quite a few of my fellow enlistees. That would probably change dramatically when they got to basic training. As I looked around at the group I wondered how some of these guys would make it in the military. I also wondered how some of them got that far in the first place. Included in this mass of people were those with many differing temperaments. Talk about a wide range of mental acuity, there were guys who were talking to themselves, and sometimes having arguments. Others were wide-eyed and appeared as though they would "go postal" at the drop of a hat. I mean no disrespect to the employees of the United States Postal Service; they do a fine job, in my opinion. However, there has been enough trouble at post offices nationwide by postal employees that the phrase "go postal" has taken on a definition of its own. So, I use it here to make a point.

On the other end of the personality spectrum, some guys looked as though they had just been delivered by the family chauffeur and were all dressed up in their Sunday best. Clearly some of these men were from well-to-do families. It was like a Hollywood film featuring the young rich kid sitting next to the homicidal maniac who is waiting for a chance to beat or kill someone for the guys back home. And, of course, there were the types like myself. I was pretty close to perfect (of course, that is my take on it) but lacking in some respects. They had come from nameless little villages in Michigan, Ohio, or other locales in the Great Lakes area.

After the first day's events we were sent home to await orders directing us to report. On the way home mom and I discussed what I had been through that day and what the future held for me. She was glad I had joined the US Navy because the odds of going to Vietnam were slimmer than they would have been if I had joined the US Army. Although the conversation was light, the fact that I was leaving home for good weighed on both of us. I am sure she was worried that one of her babies was leaving the nest. As for me, I was just plain worried. I wondered if I had made the right decision in entering military service. Would I have what it takes to make it? Fear of the unknown was eating at the two of us. We went home and returned to our daily lives and waited. The weather was perfect that year from the day of my physical until the day I reported for basic training. It was like having two separate summers to me.

During the period between the physical and the report-for-active-duty date, I conducted a lot of self-reflection on my life. Where was I coming from, where was I going, what were my goals? At the ripe old age of eighteen I really had no goals to speak of. The last two years of high school were not my most stellar. My folks were divorcing, we made a major move from Southern California to Michigan, and, to be truthful, I was the typical teenager who thought he knew everything. Of course, I really did know more than most people. These were tumultuous years for me, and I needed to get away from it all. So, in the summer of 1969 I made the fateful decision to join the navy. Trust me when I say that joining the US Navy certainly got me away from it all.

Going for a college degree was never an option for me in those days. To be certain, there was no money for that type of expenditure. However, given the last two dismal school years I had just completed, additional schooling would have been a waste of time and resources. I was definitely not interested in any more schooling. Imagine how surprised I was when the first thing the US Navy did after I completed basic training was to send me to an "A" school in Great Lakes, Illinois. Each rating, in my case Electrician's Mate, has schooling available. Class "A" school would be the beginners in that rate. Class "B" and Class "C" schools are follow-up classes for the more knowledgeable sailors from the fleet. I would eventually get a college degree, but that would have to wait until I retired from the navy.

The choice of armed forces branch to select was never a question for me. My father spent time on the submarine USS *Seahorse (SS-304)* in the South Pacific during World War II, and my brothers and I got a good dose of navy stories while growing up. I have developed

7

a few sea stories during my own career to tell my descendants too. In addition to my father's service, two of my uncles had also served in the navy during the war, and another uncle flew with the Army Air Corps until he was shot down and ended up spending time as a prisoner of war (POW) with the Germans. I can only guess what that must have been like. My older brother before me had attempted to join the military a few times but was not approved due to health issues. Joining up and serving the country was almost a rite of passage for me. Later my younger brother would serve a few years too.

Going-away party the evening before leaving for basic training.

On the November day we actually departed for basic training in Great Lakes, Illinois (GLakes), the weather across the area was clear and very cold. Again my mother had to get me to Fort Wayne at some ungodly hour in the morning. On this trip, however, my two brothers were with us. There would be no need for mom to stay that day. In the predawn darkness I said my good-byes to the family, got out of the car, and started walking toward the gate. As an afterthought

I turned around and told mom to "have supper ready when I get home." I guess it must have sounded pretty cool at the time. There I was leaving home for the first time, and I probably thought a flippant remark would seem macho. It was not macho I was feeling in the pit of my stomach. Just so you know, supper was ready for me when I returned from boot camp. Actually it was a big party with all the fixings. The "hero from boot camp" had come home.

After that brief remark I turned and, without looking back, walked through the gate. The minute I was on post I started to get another uncomfortable feeling in my belly. What was I getting myself into? Everything I could see from the gatehouse was cold, dark, and unwelcoming. The family that I had felt, as a teenager, I no longer needed, had gone. I was now alone to make it or break it on my own. I had no idea what the future held, but I was facing it on my own terms.

The day I reported for duty was as busy as the day I had come here for my physical. It included more medical tests, physical tests, and a myriad of forms to fill out and sign. A couple of months had passed since the initial physical, and they were checking to see if anything had changed. I am sure others drank as much as I did during that period, and teenagers can get into trouble and get injured. The thing I remember most about that day was that it was the day I got my first screwing from the navy. It was a red-letter day in my life, to be sure. I received a firsthand lesson on the pitfalls of believing everything you hear. More on that learning experience later.

I thought the first visit had included anything that could possibly be done in preparation for basic training. I was wrong, and it turned out to be a really long day. We moved from room to room within the facility. In each room we were tested in some way, and in a few we were asked a number of questions. Maybe this was a last-chance attempt to separate the mentally unprepared. They missed me, and I got in.

All of us were anxious to get on with serving in the military. So far, everything we did seemed to impede our progress. In reality it made no sense for us to get agitated doing what we were doing. We were theirs to do with what they would. Recruits, minions, slaves, no difference, we were in for the long haul, and it all counted on twenty. I did not know it then, but every minute I was there was another minute counted toward twenty years and retirement. It would be four years and a decision to re-up (reenlist) before that phrase meant anything to me. That initial day continued in this fashion until after the evening meal.

To end the day's proceedings, we were ushered into a room large enough to handle everyone and given the Oath of Enlistment. I remember that at that time, as happened for the following four reenlistments, I got goose bumps. I know that it sounds like I am "eaten up with it," but the Oath of Enlistment, the Chiefs Creed, "The Star Spangled Banner," and all the rest of that patriotic stuff, to this day, still mean something to me. The Pledge of Allegiance is important, and it irritates me to no end when I hear about someone burning an American flag. But that is another whole story and should wait for another time.

In 1969 the US Navy had three basic-training locations. San Diego, Waukegan, and Orlando each had a large navy presence within a larger base in addition to the basic-training facilities. My group was given the choice of San Diego or Waukegan, better known as Great Lakes Naval Training Center. Those going to California would have to fly, and the Illinois sailors were to be bussed. I do not remember Florida being an option for us. The men were fairly evenly divided on the choice. But not many really wanted to complete thirteen weeks basic during the winter months in Great Lakes. The warmer climate of Southern California seemed a much better prospect. So, we were divided into two groups. The Illinois bunch was mustered on the left side of the auditorium and the California boys on the right side. That was port and starboard to the more seasoned recruit.

I had gone to school in the San Diego area and still had some friends there, so I went to the right side. It turned out to be the wrong side. After the two groups said their bye-byes, handshakes given and kisses blown, the left side was taken to Detroit Metro Airport for the flight to San Diego, and my group on the right side was marched onto three buses waiting to take us on the six-hour ride to Illinois. We were all going in the opposite direction than we had requested. Yes, we were stunned by this surprising turn of events. As we filed out of the building into the bitter cold we heard a couple of the petty officers yell after us.

"Hey, that's your first navy fuck-job; it won't be your last! Ha-ha." They were laughing hysterically. They turned out to be prophets.

The Greyhound bus trip to Great Lakes was uneventful. The ride was a long six hours, and it was hard to sleep, even though the civilian bus driver suggested that we should. Having made this run before, he knew that we would arrive late and not be given much sleep once there. But, everyone on the bus was nervously anxious about the immediate future. We had no idea what to expect, so we were living in the fear of the unknown. That also made it very hard to rest, and, in addition, there were those on the bus who acted as though they were in the local McDonald's play area, if McDonald's had had play areas then. They were like eighteen-year-olds who had not reached puberty yet. In the next twenty-two-plus years I would meet plenty of that type. Some would have commissions, and some of those would be fairly senior. So I just sat there in the midst of all the noise on the bus with my eyes shut and kept my thoughts to myself.

Eventually the bus did quiet down, and most of the group slept or at least sat silently for the duration of the ride. Sometime after midnight, or to get it correct, approximately zero dark thirty hours, we arrived at the gate to Great Lakes Naval Training Center. The fun was just beginning. The yelling would not stop for the next thirteen weeks.

The very first up close and personal look at a United States Marine I ever had was at that moment. The bus came to a gate and stopped, the door swung open, and living hell entered our lives. A marine sentry stepped onto the bus and looked at us silently for a moment. Then he opened his mouth, and we must have all gone dumbstruck. The sound he emitted was so unrelated to anything we had ever heard that it took a few seconds before we realized that there were actually words involved, and indeed he was sending a message our way.

When we started to understand what he was saying the first words we could make out were things like maggots, mother fuckers, boot camps, shitheads, pussies, and then there were those that I never really recognized. Hey, I thought Pinckney, Michigan, had all the required swear words, but apparently there were a lot more I had never heard before. Look, my reeducation was already beginning.

A marine standing guard duty is always dressed smartly, and in a military fashion. Every article of his clothing was starched and pressed. Anything on his uniform that could be polished was brightly shining. From his hat, or cover, to his spit-polished shoes, he was the perfect example of the US Marine. He was a man to be feared.

The marine's first mistake was expecting us to vacate the bus in an orderly fashion. He wanted kids from Pinckney, Michigan, and kids from inner-city Detroit working together, oh yeah, right. The recruits on the bus, including myself, were scared. Many of them were huddled in the back of the bus hoping their newly found belief in prayer would set them free of the impending doom. Others were trying to find the back door of the bus, but there was only the restroom, and not many could hide in there at one time. You would be surprised to see how many found a seat they could squeeze under. However, the marine had seen that trick in the past and found each and every one of them anyway.

Before I knew it, I was outside the door standing in the freezing air. No, I was not particularly brave, nor did I want to meet the drill sergeant any quicker than I had to. Some of my fellow travelers were in such a hurry to get away that they pushed me right past the bus driver, who was laughing uncontrollably, and out the door. Once outside there were other marines helping out. The place was crawling with them. It was getting real scary. It was not their first rodeo, and they stood fast. In pretty short order they had us all in a line three abreast and at varying degrees of attention. It was cold outside, and we were tired, but our night was far from over.

As soon as things settled down a bit the marines stopped yelling, and we got very quiet except for the muffled sounds of sobbing in the rear of the group. The marines took a muster by calling out names and waiting for the reply "here!" Everyone was present and accounted for this fine November morning. It must have been some sort of marine punishment to be assigned here and have to try and march future sailors. In my entire career I have never seen a marine really get sailors to truly march properly. The first attempt at marching us must have looked pretty funny. I do not know for a fact, however, because I was busy staring at the back of the head in front of me. That is what we were ordered to do. We were supposed to glue our eyes to the back of the head in front of us. They first marched us to a building not far from the gate. It was painful sneaking a look back and seeing the Greyhound bus turn around and head back for Detroit. Each one of us wanted to get back on it and ride back home.

Upon entering the building each man was given a small, flattened cardboard box. Then we filed into the next room, where the marines stopped, and the petty officers started. They had new faces and different uniforms, but it was the same routine. The yelling continued.

The building we entered was nice and warm when we first got there. After a while it began to get hot. We still wore the clothes that we came in with. Everyone was bundled up for the cold Midwest winter. And some, including me, were sweating profusely. It was warm in there for a good reason. On the floor, painted in white, were approximately 150 small squares. Each square was numbered sequentially. We marched into the room and landed on a square with a number based upon where we were in the line. There were about seventy men taking up that many squares. Each square was about eighteen inches on the sides.

When we stood on our square we started getting orders to strip completely. I just knew this was going to be fun. Once naked, the order was given to place all clothes and other personal items into our boxes. Tape, pens, and labels were then handed out. We promptly stuffed all our worldly belongings we had brought with us into the box and taped it shut. Still without clothes we put the addressed label on the box. Those boxes would reach home way before we did again, and their trip would be a lot smoother. We then lined up and were ushered into the next room. The boxes were left on the squares, and we never saw them again. As we passed into the following room it was apparent that this was a symbolic out-with-the-old and into a whole new life. We left civilian life naked and entered navy life naked. You might say we were newborns to, what would be, for us, a brave new world.

When going into the clothing room we were asked our sizes of pants, shirts, dress and work shoes, and our skivvies. In reply to your answer you would get some item of clothing thrown in your face. A couple pairs of pants, shirts, and socks, with a pair of shoes, were the things I can remember. This first issue of uniform items would be a complete and heavy seabag. When you considered everything it would take to make it through basic, the pile looked pretty daunting. We were given everything from a bar of soap and soap dish to watch cap and peacoat.

Later we found that much of the uniform pieces were not the size we had indicated. The shoes fit because they would be needed in marching through training. When we finished going through the first part of the building we ended up in another room with squares on the floor. It could have actually been the room we were in before, only after our civvies were removed. On the squares, and without infringing on your neighbor's square, we got dressed in our first military uniform.

Even as late, or early, as it was, there were still things we had to accomplish before going to bed, or hitting the rack. We crammed our possessions into the seabag that was part of the original fit out. The seabag was heavy, and they took a minute to show us how to carry the bag on our shoulders. We needed bedding to make our racks in the barracks. By this time it was finally time to sleep. Every man was very tired. In the barracks we put the bedding on the bunk bed, or rack, as they are known in the navy, under the critical eye of the petty officers (PO). At zero three fifteen we could finally climb into the bed. The POs told us to go right to sleep in preparations for a big day tomorrow. I was so tired that I did go right to sleep and felt as though I slept like a log, and for a long time.

At zero three thirty, fifteen minutes later, someone threw a trashcan, or shit can, down the length of the barracks as an alarm clock for reveille. That turned out to be one of the shortest nights in my life. So, with less than fifteen minutes of sleep, our days of basic training began. Within a few hours we were skilled at getting up and dressed very fast, making our racks so a quarter would bounce on it very fast, and eating very fast, and we had been rendered bald at the barbershop. The haircut was very fast too. The barber had the courtesy to at least *ask* how we wanted our hair cut. A couple guys jokingly said, "Take it all off!" What an understatement.

A couple days later I was pulled from my original unit for a special company that was in the process of being formed. I was immediately assigned to the *Peoria Company*. This set me back about a week in my training. Our company commander (CC) had arrived too. He was a Gunner's Mate, Guns, First Class (GMG1), or Guns. He was in a perpetually foul mood because we had entered his life and were now straining his patience. Apparently, we could do nothing right. His job was to teach us how to walk and to talk, and how to think. He would be responsible for the type of sailor we were when we finally made it to the fleet.

The USS *Peoria* (*LST-1183*) was a new ship looking for a crew. Someone had the bright idea of manning the ship with guys from Peoria, Illinois, and if there were not enough recruits who wanted to then they would draw from the whole state of Illinois until they had an entire crew. They did not get enough volunteers for the ship from the city or the state, so they decided to draw recruits from the entire Great Lakes area. That is how I ended up in Company 695, the *Peoria Company*. The ship was commissioned on February 21, 1970, and was sunk as a target on July 12, 2004, after a distinguished career.

The ship was sponsored by the Navy Club of Peoria, Illinois. They sent a ship's flag, and we all signed it, even though some of us were not going to be assigned to her. They promised that the flag would be prominently displayed in a case by the door. They also said that there was a free drink waiting for each of us. I have no idea how many of us in Company 695 actually got assigned to USS *Peoria*. One thing I thought was cool about this effort was that everybody in our company was from the Midwest and had things in common. I never did get the promised drink.

Chapter 2

"You're STUPID!"

One of the first jobs a Company Commander (CC) has is to set up a command structure for the company. He sees the individuals in action during the first few days and picks out those he thinks might work out as his recruit officers. One position he has to fill is the Recruit Petty Officer in Charge (RPOC). This man will be in charge when the CC is away. The RPOC is the top dog, big banana of recruits. There is also an assistant RPOC, a Company Clerk, and Master-at-Arms, and so on. When he picks you for a position you generally feel pretty honored. This is your first opportunity to show leadership ability because you were chosen to be a Recruit Petty Officer (RPO).

A number of those chosen let the position go right to their heads. Some of them who were picked turned out to be conceited, pushy guys. It is not a chapter of basic that I reflect upon fondly. In the evening after the CC went home for the day, the RPOs would hold additional school call for the few recruits who were not progressing very well in their training. This extra training was usually pretty physical, sometimes to the point of being abusive. It mainly consisted of a lot of calisthenics to the point of exhaustion; however, it would sometimes become more personally rough. Expanding on that is not my intention here, so I will move on.

I continued through training without problems and was never singled out for extra attention, but I took notice of what was going on and never forgot what I saw happening. I am sure that the experience helped shape the petty officer that I became in the future.

In any case, Guns went about his job finding those recruits who seemed mature enough to be relied upon and that displayed leadership qualities. I was working in my stay-a-part-of-the-wall mode, and he never looked at me as a candidate for anything. But that is probably what tripped me up in the long run. He went through his list and realized that I had not applied for anything. Once I was found out, there was no getting around it. I would have to be considered for something. Was this the beginning of my leadership skills?

My big test was for the Cleaning Gear Locker Petty Officer position. I guess it was the last position to fill. The CC got three of us together to test us and to see if one of us had what it took to be the CGLPO. Just joking, there is no acronym like that. But someone did have to be assigned to the cleaning gear locker. When he was ready the CC told me to go into the gear locker, really a closet, and memorize where everything was. He shut the door and left me in there for about five minutes. Inside the cleaning gear locker were multiple shelves with various supplies stowed on them. The standard equipment for housekeeping, such as brooms, mops, buckets, dusting materials, and the like, was also there. No vacuum cleaner, however; that would be too easy.

Shortly, he let me out, went inside himself and closed the door. From outside I could hear things being moved around inside or maybe just being played with. After a few minutes he again switched places with me and told me to put everything back the way it had been originally. Once inside I just moved a few items to a different spot, made a little noise as I did, and came out. After going in and inspecting my work, he returned with a sneer-contorted face. I remember that we saw this face a lot. With the nasty smirk still in place he said to me, "You're STUPID!" He found his Cleaning Gear Locker Petty Officer in someone else, and I faded back into the wallpaper.

Every day we were given classes in the way the navy operated. You have probably heard the old adage, "There's your way, there's my way, there's the right way, and then there is the *navy way*!" In order to survive your tour of duty, you must learn the navy way. We were schooled in things such as ship maneuvering, navy nomenclature (navy terms), watchstanding, navy and military life in general, and the Uniform Code of Military Justice or the UCMJ.

The latter one is the basis of the military justice system. All members of all branches of the armed services fall under its jurisdiction. Only a few people can quote very much of this large document, and they are generally those in the legal professions. However, many sailors, if not all, can quote one line. That line is "Penetration, however slight, is sufficient to complete the offense." The line is part of the UCMJ articles concerning rape and other sexual crimes. The seriousness of such crimes aside, this line is used in a gallows humor way. Every sailor who retains the mind-set of a juvenile will always remember this line.

Our schooling in the various subjects was really more of an exposure to the concepts. Once your rate was determined, the specialized Class "A" School and training in the fleet would bring you up to speed. Whenever a test was given to see what aptitude we had, I was careful when I excelled and when I did not. I remember the radioman test. Sitting in a classroom wearing headphones, we were to listen to sounds and push the button to distinguish whether it was a dot or a dash. The constant increasing and decreasing of the various tones, dots, and dashes were making me crazy. There was no way I wanted to do this for a living, so I just pushed the buttons in a random order. When that test was over I had done so poorly that they would never let me anywhere near communications equipment.

Here's a quick mention of the type of training we received in the barracks at night from the company commander. I swear to you that this is what we did. In order to fit your uniform items into the compact lockers you have onboard ship, it is suggested that your clothing be folded the navy way. October 13, 1775, is listed as the birthday of the US Navy. Since that day, through trial and error the navy has developed procedures for just about any type of evolution you can imagine. Folding your uniform items is no exception.

Skivvies have to be folded just so and placed into that section of the locker that has been designated for that purpose. If the directions call for the waistband to be facing out of the locker, then that is how each item is placed. Every piece of clothing and uniform is treated that way. Folding your underwear in that fashion is doing it the navy way. No other way is acceptable. The navy way is prescribed for everything in the service. If it is not the US Navy way then it is not the right way.

We had clothes-folding training at night. Ironing would have made the folding easier, but irons were not issued with our seabags Since we had no irons available we were given a substitute in the form of a soap dish with a very hot washcloth inside it. The logistics of keeping the cloth inside the soap dish hot were almost impossible. Even at the hottest point this procedure failed to produce any kind of a reputable crease. We kept busy in this fashion while we learned other precious housekeeping tricks.

Another useful trick they taught us was the futility of trying to open the lock on your locker using just your nose. If you were caught away from your locker and the padlock was not locked, the punishment was to display your physical prowess by unlocking your now locked combination padlock while in the one-arm push-up position. The combination lock was placed on the deck facing up, and you could only use your nose. It was humorous watching guys give it the old college try, but I do not think anyone ever accomplished the feat. I was lucky enough to not get caught. This was simply an exercise to get you into the habit of ensuring your locker on board ship was always locked in your absence. Stealing from a shipmate is almost as bad as murder, but there are those who will still try it.

In basic training the only rest time we got was on Sunday mornings. But you were encouraged to attend Sunday services. I actually attended a service or two. It got you out of the barracks, and it was not so bad in a gymnasium setting. The Catholic Chaplain held confessions out in the open outside the hearing of others, but there were no dividers. Aside from that it was church as usual. That was pleasant enough, but Sunday had a dark side too.

We ate breakfast every morning, but on the Sabbath we returned to the barracks to relax and enjoy the Sunday Chicago papers. Any other day we would start our training for the day right after morning meal. Everything we did was on a time schedule. We got up on time, we went to bed on time, and on Sunday we moved our bowels on time. That was the first signs of future teamwork. Everybody lined up outside the head and waited their turn at a toilet. There were ten commodes for about seventy-five guys. The head had no door on it, and there were no stalls in the room. So while you waited for your seat you got a floor show for entertainment.

Ten guys sitting on the toilet with everybody else watching is not as fun as it might sound. I am a private person when it comes to the bathroom. I am not delicate; I am just private. Evidently, there are people who are not so private with their personal business. Most men get in, do what they need to do and leave. Some guys try to gross out all the others. Rigorously scratching their privates is popular with some. Then there is the guy who raises himself up enough so others can see and count the number of turds he drops. That is certainly one of my favorites. I will spare you the farting habits on display. Suffice it to say that if you are number fifty or above in line, you are not going to breathe well. Some guys never tire of such antics and keep them up until the completion of basic. Then they take their show on the road to the fleet.

The main naval base was referred to as "Main Side," and the recruit area was called "Recruit Side." Any time a company moved from place to place on either side they were marched. The two areas were separated by a public road and connected by a tunnel under that road. Each time a unit marched through the tunnel it sang "Anchors Aweigh" as loudly as possible. Somehow, the acoustics of the tunnel made the song sound good.

Some days to stay warm during transit we marched double-time. After getting there double-time, as fast as we could go, we would then invariably have to wait for whatever reason we had come for. We may have come here for extra equipment, a class in navy life, or even medical visits. So our life was filled with a lot of hurry-up-and-wait situations. Whenever a recruit company waited in line for something they were told to get as close to the man in front as they could. Sailors monitoring our progress constantly barked orders at us, saying simply, "nuts to butts, nuts to butts." A few clowns took the order seriously, got too close, and were politely but firmly rebuffed by the sailor in front of them. That was probably one of the most used phrases in the US Navy during my earlier career.

Guys being guys, sailors being sailors, and human nature being what it is, I learned early in my career that if a guy gooses your rear-end, lean back into it. If you jump, they will never stop goosing you. I have seen a case on one of my ships where it got so bad that the victim was in a constant state of jitters waiting for the next goose to come. He became so agitated that he had to be placed on antidepressant medicine to control his jumpiness. The rest of the command was given a direct order to stop goosing him. In the lines in basic there were no orders yet, so the grab-assing was constant as long as the CC could not see it. I can state honestly that I never had the desire to goose a shipmate. But I have leaned into quite a few. I guess I have, or had, a pretty attractive butt.

Anyone who has ever spent time in Great Lakes during the winter can attest to the very cold conditions. On at least two mornings we skipped breakfast due to the severe cold and how dangerous the wind chill would be if we marched in it. The company usually made all our commitments even though the snow and icy conditions made marching hazardous to even the most disciplined soldiers. However, every day my company would march out to classes at locations throughout the recruit side of Great Lakes. Marching three abreast up and down the icy roads was not my idea of a fun time.

One day we happened to be en route to the indoor gun range, which required a left turn at the bottom of a small decline with a stop sign. Normally, we would come to a halt at the sign and post guards to stop traffic. This would allow us to march out and to the left without any danger from passing vehicles. During the marches the CC always marched alongside the company about halfway back. We had been to the gun range before with no incidents.

This time at the bottom of the hill, when the CC yelled "Company, HALT!" someone in the first row, or maybe all three, slipped on the ice. As they started to lose their footing they instinctively flung an arm out to catch themselves on the buddy next to them. If he was not already falling himself, this started him on the way. The three recruits behind them started to slip when they tried to avoid getting slammed in the head by the barrel of the weapons the first three were carrying. Of course, this caused a domino effect that left practically the entire company sprawled on the ground. Confusion ensued from then on. The CC was right on top of the situation. The last thing he needed was for another CC or, worse, his own boss to see the entire company sliding around on their backs. With a lot of yelling and cursing he got us on our feet, and we continued the march shortly after the catastrophe. It seems like a relatively minor thing. However, I cannot help but think how hysterical we must have appeared to any observers.

During basic training, dental and medical visits took up a lot of our time. Many Americans around my age did not have medical or dental insurance. Policies like those available today did not exist. I spent a good deal of time in the recruit dental offices. I always felt that I was the practice part of the term "dental practice." It seemed like I was in the dental unit two to three times a week. Medical tests and exams were frequent as well.

The navy does not want to send sailors to the fleet unless they are in the best physical condition possible. All vaccinations had to be updated as well as tests taken for things such as venereal disease. To get vaccinated the whole company formed in a line and walked down a narrow corridor. Many of the buildings on the recruit side of Great Lakes were old and in some disrepair. But they were still usable for training recruits and administering medical care.

On one particular day vaccinations were given by using the fairly new jet injector gun. I had never seen or heard of the contraption before. The injector gun uses high-pressure air in conjunction with a delivery fluid to penetrate the skin and supply the medicine. The high-pressure stream of fluid breaks the skin and does the job in a second. If it sounds easier than a straightforward needle, you are wrong. But that's just my opinion. As we moved through the line and got closer to the injector gun, the operation was in full view.

Just before I got there a corpsman took a shot with the gun toward the wall. At the point of fluid impact the plaster broke and some of it fell to the floor. Now I figured that they could not be shooting the wall all the time; it would waste time, plaster, and medicine. I thought they must repair the wall before they went home in preparation for the next day's vaccination show. Real or not, it was a pretty good show for those of us getting shots. It gave us something to think about as we got closer to the dreaded injector gun. We all got quiet and thought about what the gun would do to our arms.

I, for one, did not have much meat on the bones of my upper arms. When I finally arrived in the position for my first injection I was told not to flinch or move my arm in any way. If the shot is given at an angle, the result can be a mild to serious cut in the flesh. It was not to be taken lightly. I braced myself for the shock, and when it came I almost fell with the pain. I was surprised that the fluid did not go completely through my arm and lodge in my side. We each got a couple of shots administered in both arms in quick succession. We were relieved when it was over. Then, much to our chagrin, we saw two more guns farther down the line.

Stories from basic training would fill a multivolume set of books. Each company has around seventy-five men, and each of them has their own physical and mental baggage to carry with them. Coming from different backgrounds meant a multitude of morals and attitudes. Men from the various parts of the country had different terms and habits then those from other areas. I remember the first time I heard a guy say, "I can't wait until I'm home and can chase some cock!"

He was originally from Texas and still ended up in the *Peoria Company*. After he had made the comment he noticed that we were all staring at him and some had moved away from where he sat.

"What's wrong with you guys?" He still did not understand why we stared at him.

Finally one of my friends explained the difference, to most of us, between the word *cock* and the word *pussy*. Where he came from, the two words were synonymous. As I have indicated, every day was another learning experience.

Proper watchstanding was another important lesson in basic training. Here I am standing watch over the rest of the company while they slept.

But this prepared us for the fleet. I survived basic training relatively unscathed because I had stayed part of the wallpaper; I blended into my surroundings, and did not draw attention to myself. At the end of training we had to work off all the demerits we had been awarded since day one.

Demerits were given to a recruit for any number of infractions, such as leaving your personal locker unlocked, shoes not shined properly, or even falling asleep in class. If you did fall asleep in class the instructor would throw an eraser at you, and they were all crack shots. *Bam*, they hit you right in the head. When the final tally was totaled everyone in the company had more demerits than I did. I only had two. Well, the CC would have none of that. He immediately gave me about fifteen demerits for just being ugly. My punishment was to duckwalk around the clotheslines outside in the courtyard of the barracks. Duckwalking and quacking like a duck while holding your rifle across your back from shoulder to shoulder on ice and snow in freezing temperatures SUCKS.

Between the duckwalk and going home was our final week and official graduation from basic training. The graduation ritual was held on Friday, February 6, and was attended by a number of dignitaries—none of whom I knew. Well, one was the Chief of Naval Operations (CNO) Thomas H. Moorer, and I had a vague idea who he was. After all I had just gone through thirteen weeks of naval basic training. The important attendees to us, the recruits, were our families in the crowd. My mother bore four boys into this world, one of whom only lived a few hours, and I was the middle of the three left. I come from a family with a proud military background. My brothers and I were all honored by the service of our father and uncles, and now I was going into the service.

My parents were divorced, and my father was a long-haul trucker who was not close enough to attend the graduation ceremony. My mother, older brother, and his wife, along with my younger brother, drove the almost three hundred miles from Pinckney, Michigan, to Great Lakes, Illinois, to attend the ceremony. For me they would be a welcome sight.

The recruits were in the barracks busying themselves trying to get everything just right on their uniforms. There were probably seven or eight more companies involved in the day's festivities, and because of that there were a bunch of guys running around the berthing areas in all stages of getting ready. After what seemed like hours we were told to muster with weapons on the asphalt grinder next to the building. Proper navy nomenclature for the asphalt is "grinder." Do not ask why it is called that; just take my word for it."

The recruit side of the Naval Training Center was pretty secure and off-limits to unauthorized persons. We certainly felt as though we were trapped within the perimeter. Well, imagine my surprise when going out the barracks door I bumped into my two brothers as they were coming in. I can think of probably three spots from the front gate to the back of the facility where our barracks were that security should have stopped them, should have maybe arrested them. Later, when we could have a cold beer and talk, they explained that as the crowd came through the gate they simply peeled off the group and headed towards the barracks. They knew they were looking for Company 695 so they walked and waited until they saw what turned out to be a recruit from another company and asked for directions. That was almost their downfall. When asked, the recruit said, "Company 695? Ah, yeah, first deck, portside, forward."

This made my brothers look at each other and say, "*What?*" They kept walking and asked a couple more times until they found my berthing.

When I saw them I felt like laughing and crying. I was glad to see them, but since they had broken security I could see a lot more duckwalking in my immediate future. After we said our hellos I had to muster, and they made their way to the rest of the families. I remember thinking, "Only my brothers could or would do that." The rest of the day went without a hitch.

At the end of basic, each sailor was given two weeks of leave from the navy. Friday, February 13, was the first time I came home in uniform, and my mother was impressed (oh, ma) even if no one else was. I spent those two weeks just fooling around. The day I came home the weather was beautiful—clear, sunny, and cold. I did not mind the cold air and snow on the ground. I was just glad to be home in familiar surroundings, with family and friends. I spent my leave visiting people and being invited to dinner. I was the first in the clan to serve in the military since the World War II generation, and that was twenty-three years ago.

Chapter 3

"Your nose to the hose."

When my two-week leave at home was over, I traveled back to Great Lakes to attend Electrician's Mate Class "A" School. I enjoyed this tour at the Naval Training Center much more than the first one. This time I was on the Main Side. I could come and go as I wanted and even have a life off base as long as it was legal and did not interfere with my studies. As I said before, after high school I was in no mood to continue my education. However, this course was different than anything I had come across before. These instructors could keep me after class any time they wanted. Every assignment they gave was considered a lawful order. If you did not maintain a decent grade point average they forced you into evening study or, as we called it, "stupid study." Too bad civilian teachers do not have that kind of control over their students.

Here, as before, my grades were not stellar, but I kept them high enough to graduate on time. I also left Great Lakes as an E-3 in rank. When you completed "A" school you were advanced to that rank and given the rating insignia to wear with it. My friends and I were strutting around the barracks like little peacocks showing our new colors. That was okay, however, because when we got to the fleet we would find that E-3 meant nothing to real sailors, and no strutting was allowed.

After completing school in Great Lakes I received my orders. During the first week of August 1970 I was traveling again. First I went to Newport Naval Station and then, a week later, to Quonset Point Naval Air Station, both in the Narragansett Bay area of Rhode

Island. Again I found myself under official orders and took them seriously. Official orders always state that the service member is to depart and arrive at a certain time using phrases like "on or about," "not later than," "not earlier than," and so on. They pretty much have it all covered. So, I had to leave my family and friends in Michigan and report for duty. I was ready to leave and kind of excited about going to my first real command.

My first real naval command, from 1970 to mid-1972, would be the USS *Wasp (CVS-18),* homeported in Quonset Point, Rhode Island. The *Wasp* was a World War II Essex-class aircraft carrier, primarily involved in anti-submarine warfare (ASW) operations. En route to *Wasp* I had a temporary stop in Newport, Rhode Island, for one week of firefighting school at Newport Naval Station.

One of the most deadly occurrences on a ship at sea is fire. Aircraft carriers are very susceptible to onboard fires because of all the aircraft fuel they carry. When a ship is at sea a fire onboard is about as serious as it can get. The ship is the only place there is. If you lose it to a fire, you will be swimming. Fires can strike fast and be extremely deadly. I do not believe anything can prepare you for a shipboard or an aircraft fire. The closest thing there is has got to be firefighting school. In boot camp I was briefly exposed to fires and fighting them. But that is just a quick introduction to the fire. It cannot prepare you for the intense heat or the thick black smoke an oil fire conjures up. Only the school can do that, and they do an excellent job of it.

The Naval Education and Training Center (NETC), where I completed my first real firefighting class, was located in Newport, and was also the home of Officer Candidate School (OCS). I was there in mid-August 1970 and the temperatures were in the high 90-degree range. I remember it was very hot. At the Firefighting Training Center were buildings with mock-ups of ship engines, boilers, and machinery spaces. Outside were pools of water and an area to practice flight deck firefighting techniques. Various types of fire suppression equipment were located at stations around the facility. All these assets were put to good use. One of the big lessons I got here was experiencing the intense heat from being so close to the fire.

After some class work for about one half of a day, we went outside and got down to setting and extinguishing real fires. Did I say "real"? Oh boy, they were real enough to get some students and instructors slightly injured.

There were two fires that I distinctly remember because of the valuable lessons I learned while fighting them. The first was a simulated engine room fire. Picture a three-story building with nothing inside but steel grating catwalks, ladders, and assorted obstacles. The floor can be seen thirty feet below through the decking. But what you cannot see at first is that the floor is really nothing but an empty pool that could hold water or any liquid, like, for instance, oil. When everyone has been briefed and is ready, the instructors let oil into the pool at the bottom of the building. The firefighting team has already been placed at the top on a catwalk just outside one of the entry hatches. The second they set fire to the oil in the pool, huge billows of black smoke and soot rise up and expel from any opening available. Along with it comes the intense heat. Our job then becomes entering via the hatch and fighting our way across catwalks and down ladders to put out the inferno.

Imagine that you are cooking steaks on the grill. When the coals are as hot as they ever get, place a small man about three inches high onto the grill. Tell him to climb down inside the barbecue and put out the fire. That is exactly what we are attempting at the top of the building. To this day I cannot stand near anyone grilling meat and not think of this fire. The building is the grill, the oil at the bottom is the charcoal and, of course, we are the meat.

The first thing to dawn on you is the terrible fact that you cannot breathe intense heat and thick soot. A human body is just not built that way. The heat burns your lungs, and the soot covers you, inside your lungs and outside in a thick coating, and even your eyes start to develop a layer of soot on them. For this fire we were not given the equipment available to damage control teams onboard ship. We were not using the oxygen breathing apparatus (OBA). That came later on during other exercises. This is why the elements of the fire were getting to us in massive quantities and making us dizzy. Firefighting without OBAs gave each student the opportunity to experience a real fire up close and personal. Believe me when I say you will not forget it very soon, if ever.

After some last-minute instructions from the staff we manned our fire hose. My position was about five men back from the nozzleman. The nozzleman would fight the fire, and the rest of us kept the hose under control. I have always had a hard time with smoke bothering me, but this was way beyond anything I had ever confronted. I was wearing a heavy and hot fireman's coat and helmet and at one point had to stop and kneel while the nozzleman did his job. He had to work the nozzle back and forth to try and push the fire away and keep it from floating underneath us. Kneeling there was agony, and I really thought I would pass out from lack of fresh air. It was at that point I remembered an incident from earlier in the day.

During the morning session I had witnessed a junior officer who was there as a student arguing with an instructor, who happened to be an enlisted man. The instructor had the same build as my future father-in-law. About five feet six and weighing around 120 pounds, he was not particularly imposing. But, also like my father-in-law, he had an attitude that gave him about three more feet of height. I have no idea what the argument was about, but if you have ever been in the navy, you can guess who won and had the last word. That is right, the instructor did. The one who assigns the grade, the one with the clipboard, is the one who is right.

Before he let the student go, I heard the instructor say, "Remember, if you can't breathe, put your nose to the hose," or words to that effect.

They went their separate ways. I saw the student throughout the day, and he turned out to be a whiner who constantly irritated the rest of us. I am not just saying that because he was an officer. Although, I think that was the root of his problem. He did not like training with us minions and bucked at taking directions from an enlisted man in front of us.

I do not remember what material the hoses were made from or how they were constructed in the '70s. They were some sort of fabric, tightly woven and manufactured into a fire hose. The hoses were not the solid rubber ones like some fire-suppression equipment used in today's navy. That is all the explanation required for my purposes. As I kneeled there thinking I was going to black out, the instructor's comment came back to me. The hose was currently not advancing, and we were kneeling and holding the hose firmly in position. My position was such that I only had to lean forward a short way to touch the hose with my nose. What an awakening that turned out to be. The second my nose met the canvas of the hose the coolest and freshest air I had ever breathed filled my lungs. Air from the water rushing through the hose was emanating from the hose's cloth jacket, and it made a layer of one and a half inches of cool, fresh air around the hose. I had never realized how great air could actually taste.

I knelt there breathing that wonderful air for as long as the nozzleman needed me to. When he had completed his actions, we moved on into the fire, creeping inch by inch until he had the fire under control or out. After his turn on the nozzle he went to the back of the line and took up a position at the rear of the hose. The next man in line then moved up to become the nozzleman, and we each moved up one station closer to the nozzle and the fire. The rest of this exercise, including me on the nozzle, was completed uneventfully.

A simulated aircraft fire provided me with the second lesson. Inside the firefighting school's compound is a round pool about fifteen to twenty feet across. A layer of water about four to six inches deep is inside the pool. A layer of oil is floated on top of the water. This is what they will ignite to start the blaze. In the center of the pool lies a helicopter mockup in the upright, or wheels-down, position. The exercise consists of the team wading through the burning oil, keeping everyone safe, rescuing a "crash test dummy" type of figure from inside the aircraft, and returning everyone back to safety. Sounds easy enough, doesn't it? Well, there are considerations to contend with.

When fighting a fire like this, the two men at the nozzle wear fire suits to protect them when wading through the flames. The suit is silver in color and looks as if it is made of aluminum foil. It is thick enough and made of fire-retardant materials to withstand great heat and still keep the wearer safe. These suits are heavy, with no airflow, and the occupants sweat profusely when wearing them. As I remember it, the goal of the fire team is to spray the flames with enough water to push the fire away from the two men in suits trying to rescue the pilot from the aircraft. This procedure clears a path so they can do their job. The trick is to not get those suits wet.

Once they are wet, the silver suits act like a pressure cooker and can literally cook the occupants. The person inside the suit must feel like a lobster. In that case, the team must keep the water spray on the suits to keep them as cool as possible. My big lesson out of an aircraft fire is that the intense heat was absolutely incredible. It was so hot I had the strongest urge to leave my hose position and run away. This was a controlled drill in a training facility. A real shipboard fire must be so much scarier.

Almost all of us got burned a little, while some students required slight medical attention. One of the worst burns was from the water retardant on our jacket hoods melting onto the tops of our ears. When I say we all got burned some, I am referring to blisters and tan-like burns on the hands and face. The team had to wade through what seemed like twenty-foot flames and slosh through the burning oil to get to the pilot of the crashed aircraft. All of us were wearing raincoats with hoods attached. The hoods got so hot that their water-resistant material was melting and dripping onto our ears, leaving everyone with varying degrees of burns.

I read once that intense heat can make your body react before you have a chance to stop it. This is used to explain one of the reasons why some victims jump from high-rise building fires. The incredible heat shocks the body into jumping away from the fire, and if the person is already at a window seeking fresh air, they are out the opening before they realize it. Also, some victims are blown out by heat and pressure changes.

When I felt the overwhelming desire to run from the heat and flames, I was in a middle position on the hose and probably could not have gotten away if I tried. So, I got myself under control, stayed with my team, helped rescue the pilot, helped put out the fire, and graduated from firefighting school. Being that close to the fire and feeling the incredible heat is something I will never forget.

Fighting fires all day long can wear a person out. I was certainly no exception. Each night I returned to the barracks hardly being able to walk. The distance between the barracks and the school was not that great, but when you are dead tired it is far enough. On one occasion I was so tired I decided to skip evening meal. After school that day I simply got undressed and sank into my rack. I slept so soundly that I did not move until the next morning. When I did wake up I felt like I had been sleeping for a very long time.

Still dazed and feeling confused, I looked at the clock on the wall and realized that I was late for breakfast, and who wants to fight fires on an empty stomach? Judging by the various stages of dressing others in the barracks were in, I figured I had time to shave at least, get dressed, and make it to school. Almost all the sinks in the head were taken so I must not have been the only sailor to get up late. When I finished in the head I hurried to my locker and started throwing clothes on.

I was still tired from the firefighting we did the day before. I was also apparently acting a little goofy. The Third Class Petty Officer (PO3) in the next bunk looked over and said something I could not understand. When I did not respond properly he again said something that I again did not understand, and this time he pointed out the window. The sun was not making very good progress in starting the day. In fact, it looked as though it had gotten closer to the horizon than higher above it. The Petty Officer asked me what day of the week it was. When I told him what day it was, he shook his head and smiling said no and that the day I picked was tomorrow.

I looked around and saw other guys settling in for the evening or getting dressed to go out or doing other things. No one looked like they were getting ready for school. I was the only one. The Petty Officer had been at his rack when I got there from school, and he noticed that I went straight to sleep. I slept like the dead. I was so worn out and tired that when I woke up after only a couple hours I felt that I had slept through the night.

The setting sun was near the horizon, and I thought it was rising. There are always people in various states of undress in the barracks, but I thought they were getting dressed for school. I was totally off in my thinking about what time it was. After laughing his head off, the Third Class told me to get undressed and go back to sleep until reveille and enjoy the extra time in the rack. As a lowly fireman I did exactly what I was told by the PO. When I got into my bunk I went right to sleep. I remember thinking that this was like getting a whole extra night to sleep. After all that, I slept pretty darn well.

Chapter 4

"They're such pussies!"

My first run-in with the US Navy Shore Patrol (SP) happened the night I graduated from firefighting school. Even today I cannot figure out how it happened. Newport was an intermittent stop on my orders. My final destination was Quonset Point Naval Air Station to await the arrival of the USS *Wasp (CVS-18)*. The ship was returning from a four-month North Atlantic cruise. Remember, I was on my own and new in the navy. I was supposed to get to Quonset and report in that evening.

Although Rhode Island is a small state, for me it may as well have been a continent. I could not find Narragansett Bay on my own, let alone find my way from Newport to Quonset Point. If you look at a map of Rhode Island you will see that the east side is mostly water, Narragansett Bay. In the future I would refer to it as Nasty-Gansett. No offense to my fellow Americans from Rhode Island.

After graduating firefighting Friday morning, I wandered around trying to figure out how to make the transit from Newport to Quonset. One of my favorite sayings I used after a few years in the navy was, "When in doubt, ask about." However, I had not yet gotten to that kind of thought process in 1970. I was not in the habit of asking too many questions for fear of being considered stupid. When I first entered the service I was just another young new recruit who was not interested in bumping into anyone senior to me, and especially someone with a commission. I was afraid of not saluting properly and getting the riot act read to me by some officer. It had already happened to me once since I joined.

During the thirteen-week vacation known as boot camp, a fellow recruit became ill and had to be hospitalized. I was in Company 695 in Great Lakes, Illinois, from November 1969 to February 1970. At that time I was a hard-charging E-1, a seaman recruit. When it came time for someone to pack up the sick recruit's personal belongings and place them into his seabag and deliver it to the Naval Hospital, I was chosen. Lucky me! I had to take his property to the hospital on the Main Side of the base. In Great Lakes a recruit sticks out among the adult population like a crow in a flock of seagulls.

This was quite an adventure for me. I had never had to use public transportation in my life. Pinckney, Michigan, probably still does not have buses. I had to figure out the base bus system and how to navigate it by myself, sans company commander for guidance, in the big world that I was no longer a part of. We saw this world through the recruit-side fence. Only one thing was very memorable about the trip to the hospital. I had made it over there, given the recruit his belongings, and spent some time sharing updates. After about twenty minutes I departed.

Now, I was standing in front of the hospital waiting for the bus to take me back to the safety of recruit side. Imagine the picture. It is in December and fairly cold in Great Lakes. The cold wind is really blowing. I am clearly a recruit with my watch cap, peacoat, earmuffs, and those extremely sexy government-issued eyeglasses with a rubber strap holding them on. Oh yeah, I am standing at attention and looking straight ahead hoping I do not make eye contact with anyone. Especially someone senior to me, and that included everyone coming and going around me.

So, there I stand minding my own business and wanting like mad to just get back to the recruit side. I was minding my own business quite well when suddenly a female lieutenant starts screaming at me as loud as she could.

"Don't they teach you to salute in boot camp anymore?" She was making quite a scene.

Of course, I almost crapped in my pants, which would cause yet another problem. The US Navy frowns on those who crap in their uniform pants. I quickly snapped a boot camp salute and stayed looking straight ahead. The lieutenant must have felt satisfied because she broke off our interaction by going along on her own business. The bus came, I went, and the cold weather hung around until spring. Nothing else was ever said, and with the exception of my career-long distrust of female officers, life continued.

No matter what I feel, there are great numbers of women who serve both as officers and enlisted who are good sailors who can be relied upon in an emergency. Women have proven beyond question that they are capable of serving in the military and excelling at their duties.

I told you that story to help explain why I was not eager to talk with anyone in Newport. It seemed like during the last few months I was always getting jumped on for something. Most of it was bull. Everybody jumps on the newbies for any reason that they can. I was tired of feeling like I was stupid all the time and adopted a habit of not asking too many questions.

So in Newport I was very gun-shy in dealings with anyone senior to me. I spent a lot of time wandering around trying to figure out what my next step should be in getting to Quonset. However, late in the afternoon I found myself sitting on a bench and talking with a Petty Officer Third Class. The conversation went all around various topics. Sitting there and talking, I began to see that this guy might be able to help me out.

I ended up telling him about the travel problem I had and that I had no money to get to Quonset. The Petty Officer helped me out by taking me to the Personnel Office. This being late Friday afternoon, the Newport Naval Base was operating with only the duty section. The officer on duty said they would get me to NAS Quonset. I had a seat in the lobby and waited. Not long after that the shore patrol showed up. They had come for me. I was told to sign some papers and the Personnel Officer was using words like "misappropriation of government funds," "failure to report," and a few others. By now I was so worried that I was really considering crapping in my pants. Crap in them on purpose.

The next step on my journey to Quonset Point was to be placed into a shore patrol paddy wagon with my seabag. I was to be part of a prisoner exchange between the two naval stations. I am a prisoner? The shore patrol drove me to the Newport side of the recently finished Newport Bridge. There the Quonset counterparts arrived with their prisoner. Since it was an expensive trip across the new bridge I guess the bases took turns paying the toll. They meet at one end and make the trades of prisoners. This time there were only two of us, one coming from each base and one going. Once I was in the wagon going to Quonset I started to assess my situation more closely. It did not take long to realize I was in a deep pile of poop-poop. I had not been in the navy a year yet and already was a prisoner.

When we got to NAS Quonset Point they stopped in front what I think was the administration building. The sailor on the passenger side unlocked the back door and took me out. They were both big guys, and one of them grabbed my seabag and carried it for me. I guess I was too slow for them. Inside, the shore patrol left me in the office of what must have been their duty officer. The man behind the desk was a Chief Petty Officer. This Chief looked pretty squared away and was in an impeccable uniform. He started going through the paperwork that I had just been delivered with. I waited for him to finish.

After a few minutes he asked me my side of the story. So, I told him. Even today, I really do not know whether I was paid in advance or what the deal was. I was right out of basic training via EM "A" school and going to my first ship. I was confused, and I remember thinking that joining the navy might not have been such a good idea.

After a short talk the man behind the desk mumbled, "They're such pussies over there!"

He then tore up the paperwork and tossed it into the wastebasket. He asked if I had had evening meal yet, because there was still time if I needed it. I was not really in the mood to eat, so he gave me my check-in papers and pointed me toward the barracks. I was finally going to get to bed. I never heard the phrase "misappropriation of government funds" again in relation to me.

The next few weeks were fairly quiet for me. I was assigned different duties each day from cutting grass to field-daying the barracks to checking ID cards to directing traffic. I really did not like the field day assignment. Field day was just a navy term for the daily cleaning of the barracks and surrounding areas. Every day the living areas of the barracks were dusted and wiped down, and the floors were stripped, cleaned, waxed, and buffed. The heads at each end were not forgotten. In addition to what was already mentioned, the toilets and sinks and showers were cleaned and shined too. The faucet handles, the shower heads and toilet handles, and anything that could shine were known as brightwork. When field day was over, the brightwork shined so much that you could use it as a mirror and shave in the reflection.

I particularly liked directing traffic during the morning and late afternoon rush hours. NAS Quonset Point was a hubbub of activity each day. The air station was home to various air wings, repair facilities, support units, and two aircraft carriers. In addition, the Davisville Naval Construction Battalion Center (NCBC) base was next door. This base was home for the US Navy Seabees. All this combined to make rush hour traffic pretty exciting when you are standing in the middle of it.

I stood my post in the middle of the main road through the facility, and being there put me in control of much of the base traffic. Dressed in whites and wearing an orange vest, complete with white gloves, guard belt, billy club or nightstick, and whistle made me feel pretty darned formidable against anything traffic could throw at me. Ah, the stupidity of youth. I can see now, from this vantage point, just how dangerous it must have really been.

Not to demean the character of anyone driving to the base each morning, but I sometimes wonder what percentage of those drivers speeding past me every day were still half in the bag from the night before. Some of them missing me by mere inches were probably still legally drunk. But the power of being a traffic cop (not really a cop) filled my head with thoughts of being in control, and I never considered how dangerous it might have been. I could even stop an admiral's car if I wanted to. I never was so bold as to do that, but I did think about it.

One evening while I waited for the *Wasp* to return from her North Atlantic cruise I walked down to the pier where she would tie up. Eventually the USS *Intrepid* would berth across the pier from my carrier. Both carriers shared the pier and periodically were tied up at the same time. I was really impressed the first time I saw them across the pier from each other.

Intrepid is the same one on display as a museum in New York City. After a long, distinguished career, the carrier was decommissioned, towed to a permanent berth, and made into a giant display for tourists. That is a great sight to see, and you should try to visit *Intrepid* at least once.

When I got to the pier it was empty, so I walked to the end of it and turned around. I do not know what caused me to want to toss every stone I found on the pier out into the water. It is a kid's thing. My sons still do it today, although we are not near a pier to speak of. On my return from the end of the pier I did throw every rock I saw into the water. It was fun.

I passed the base fire station on my way back to the barracks one day and struck up a conversation with one of the firemen outside washing one of their trucks. He was a nice guy and probably getting close to retirement age. I was there a few times, and we always talked about things in general. I am sure he did not know how much I liked those evening conversations, but they helped the time go faster in my wait for *Wasp*. Once the ship arrived and I checked aboard, I never saw the civilian fireman again. I was too busy trying to find my place among three thousand other guys.

Chapter 5

"Stay in the shop."

During the twenty-two-plus years I served in the navy I encountered a number of chaplains. These meetings were more or less beneficial to both parties. By that, I mean we both had a job to do, and we helped each other achieve good results. However, I never looked at the Chaplains Corps as the first place to go for help. I have always felt that chaplains had their place and jobs like everyone else. If asked at the time, I am sure I would have expressed the sentiment that their place was nowhere near mine. I never needed a chaplain to help me do my job. I do not mean to belittle them or sell short their great contributions to the service; this is just how I feel. For all the good they do and the great things they accomplish, chaplains, like the rest of us, have their limits too. I developed this ambivalence toward military men of the cloth while stationed aboard *Wasp*.

USS *Wasp (CVS-18)* tied to pier at Quonset Point.
Background mast is USS *Intrepid (CVS-11)*. Taken August 1970.

The *Wasp* returned from a cruise, and I checked aboard in August 1970. From the moment you check aboard a new command you automatically start eyeing those you meet to determine who may or may not be a suitable friend. The men you meet and accept as friends will have a lasting effect on your tour at that command. Anyone you choose to get close to can cast a positive or negative light on your success simply by the influence they exert on you. The man I eventually picked to hang around with was another fireman, like me. He had been aboard the *Wasp* for over a year already. Thus he knew a lot of the intricacies of living on this particular ship. In the end it turned out to be a good decision on my part to befriend him. He was a good, conscientious sailor and helped me a lot in acclimating to shipboard life.

Everyone joining the navy at that time had to determine what rate they would strive, or *strike,* for. A man's rate was his job description; in my case I was an Electrician's Mate or EM. EM can also refer to *enlisted men*, as you will see later. Striking for a rate is simply shooting for that navy occupation. The many rates one can strike for are divided into a number of major groupings.

One group is the deck ratings. Someone with my rank in the deck ratings would be a seaman. A junior working with a construction battalion would be a constructionman. A sailor working with the air wings would be an airman, and so on. I worked below decks in the Engineering Department. We were involved in a ship's main propulsion equipment.

In addition to different titles, each rating group uses colors to denote their specialty. Airman wore green ranking insignia; seaman used white, and my department, engineering, wore red. Underneath all the rating and colors is another, more basic, ranking system. Enlisted can advance through the ranks from E-1 to E-9. As a fireman I was an E-3, or one step below being a petty officer. In addition to being a fireman, my new friend was the division's leading fireman—a position that was somewhat more senior than mere fireman.

As I settled into the routine of shipboard life, our friendship continued to develop until we were close professional and personal friends. He was from a city in Massachusetts that was close enough for him to hitchhike home on the weekends. Officially, hitchhiking was frowned upon by the navy. In reality, however, transportation was at a premium for junior enlisted in the early seventies. I was invited to go with him on a couple of weekends and got to meet his wife and newborn son. We became close enough to share personal aspects of our lives. During our free time we would sit and discuss where we were and where we were going in life. It was during a session like that that I learned of a financial problem he was having.

Anyone who has ever been in the military can attest to the problems of pay that can sometimes develop. One time you are overpaid, and the next time you are underpaid. When you are underpaid it works out that it is a major problem for you, but disbursing never seems to have the time to correct it. When you are overpaid, of course, disbursing goes to general quarters (battle stations) to get you to repay all funds owed immediately. My friend was on the wrong end of the deal. He had been overpaid by quite a bit over a period of time before it was discovered. One payday he went to get paid, and there was nothing for him. After some heated discussion he learned that not only were they taking what he owed out of that payday, but they were taking at least the next payday too. In order to satisfy the debt he knew nothing about, he and his family would go more than a month without pay.

In that day and age missing one payday would spell disaster for a petty officer, let alone a fireman. The Disbursing Officer said that they were following normal procedures, and he would have to find a way through it. I bet he would not have wanted to tell that to the now one-year-old at home crying for milk. Those little rug rats never understand about not being paid. They still want that milk. Ya gotta love those little crumb chasers, don't ya?

We both worked out of the After Distribution Shop in "E" (Electrical) Division in the Engineering Department. So, after getting no assistance from disbursing, we huddled in the shop trying to figure how he was getting through more than a month without pay. I had less time in service than he did, so my pay would only help a little. In the middle of our desperate brainstorming I came up with a great idea. An idea that I got from boot camp and that I was sure would solve our problem.

I suggested we go and see the chaplain for assistance. It took a while to find the people who knew the channels for seeing the chaplain. As it turned out later, it was easier than we were told. After running around to various offices onboard *Wasp*, we were finally given the information we needed. All we really had to do in the first place was to go to the ship's library, where the chaplain had an office, and knock on the door.

The chaplain was in his office and answered the door on the first knock. Things were starting to look up, and we thought the problem would be short-lived. After about twenty minutes of explaining the situation we were in, the chaplain, a lieutenant, I believe, agreed that there was indeed a problem. He left us outside the office in the passageway while he went to talk with the Disbursing Officer. The lieutenant returned in about an hour. The news he brought with him was not good. Apparently he had talked to the "powers that be" and was convinced that they were well within their rights as the ship's disbursing office to take the pay whenever they find a problem. Therefore he could not help us against regulations. A more experienced chaplain may have returned with better news. So, after exhausting ourselves in that endeavor to no good end, we returned to the shop and our desperate huddling.

Now, to be honest, I have to say that I do not personally know whether my friend had or had not actually noticed the difference in his paycheck. In those days we were paid in cash every two weeks. Today, I think it is direct deposit once a month. That is the way it was done when I retired from the service in January 1992. Every payday we would line up at various tables based on first initial of our last name. The pay list was posted prior to the actual day and each sailor had to complete a pay chit in the exact amount on the list. It was possible to take a smaller amount than listed and let the balance ride until the following payday or even longer. This practice resulted in varying amounts due each person on payday. It was very important to keep track of your pay every two weeks so that this type of problem did not occur. Periodically disbursing would round up or down your pay to cover those pesky odd pennies. So, your pay would fluctuate from week to week.

Living hand to mouth can affect people in various ways. If my friend noticed the overpayment, and it was not all that large, he may have accepted it as fate's way of helping out his family. Maybe he thought it would never be found. I do not know what he was thinking. But I do know he was good guy, a great friend, and an honest sailor. I personally feel that disbursing has responsibility to keep better track of their funds. An E-3 in the military cannot survive that kind of mistake.

So we ended up where we had begun. We were frantically brainstorming to find a solution. We were feeling pretty desperate. We thought of all kinds of ideas between the two of us and threw them onto the table for discussion while we sat there. This happened on a Friday afternoon, so there were limited shipmates aboard whom we could ask for assistance. Due to the constant workload when a ship is at sea, most ships have liberal liberty policies while in homeport. Therefore, many of the crewmen can get Fridays off, or at least the afternoon. This was the case on the day we looked for help. Like all sailors, the Disbursing Officer and his crew wanted any time they could for personal business. The disbursing office closed at lunch, effectively cutting off any attempts we could make for a solution until Monday. We were now about as low as it gets. However, our fortunes were about to change.

Thinking back, I can truthfully say that the two of us were very agitated over the pay problem and must have looked like a couple of kids. Not long after lunch we got a visitor to the shop. Most of those still onboard *Wasp* were either living aboard, on duty, or just there for any one of a number of reasons. One of E Division's personnel who did not go home every weekend was the senior enlisted man attached. The Senior Chief Electrician's Mate (EMCS) was just making rounds of division spaces to ensure all was right in the world. EMCS Cleveland lived in upstate New York and went home about once a month. Since he was onboard he liked to keep up on things whether he had duty or not. It always seemed to me that the guys in khakis are constantly nosing into stuff just to find trouble. Years later, wearing my own khakis, I did the same thing. We were very lucky that the EMCS was in the area that day.

Senior Chief Cleveland was a decent guy and easy enough to approach. When I rate Senior Chiefs I have served with, he is on the top of the leadership ladder. I would like to think that he was at least partly responsible for the way, in the future, that I would conduct myself as a Senior Chief. As much as I liked him and as much as he had a positive effect on my navy career, I can remember a few ass-chewings I got from him. Now I know that I deserved them all. Maybe in the next book I will cover the reasons for his anger at me.

The second he entered the shop, Senior could tell something was seriously wrong. His divisional leading fireman and another fireman were obviously stressed out. They were cussing and cursing the navy, which is mainly frowned upon. So he took a break from his rounds, sat down, and listened to our story. Since it was his problem, my friend did most of the talking. While he listened, Senior's facial features took on a life of their own. They went from quizzical to concern and on to pissed off. When it was over he told us to stay in the shop, he would be back, and he left. "Stay in the shop," he had said, like we had anywhere to go or any money to do anything. We went back to brainstorming.

Around an hour later the Senior Chief returned. He had a pay chit ready for my friend to sign and told him to go to disbursing and see the guy on duty. The duty section was in the office and waiting for him. He was getting his full pay for that period, and since it was technically not his fault, I think he did not have to repay the full amount. I am not sure how it all happened, but, if I remember correctly the Senior Chief started out in the Chiefs' Mess, probably talking with the Chief Disbursing Clerk. From there it is anyone's guess. He had saved the day, and I had learned a very valuable lesson about Chaplains and Senior Chiefs—a lesson I carried with me for the duration of my navy career.

Having been involved in this episode, I was always keen to the pay situation of the troops. By that I mean I listened up whenever someone was having difficulties in that area. Not getting paid is a disaster for anyone, and even if it is not your own pay, the man working for you is distracted until his payday fiasco is solved. Another lesson I always remembered was that Senior Chiefs stick up for their troops, as do most Chiefs. Chaplains do not always have the answers. Or, at least they need more experience in some cases.

I imagine that one of the worst jobs on an aircraft carrier has got to be as a Messcook in the galley. Most junior personnel reporting spend ninety to 120 days on messcook duty. A popular euphemism for the position is "messcrank." Since I had attended Electrician's Mate Class "A" School in Great Lakes, I was a designated striker. Usually there were enough nondesignated personnel to work the galley, but sometimes there were not. Working in the galley meant some time in the cooking area and time in the dining area. The area everybody loved the most was the scullery. No matter where you were assigned, the galley was open on a carrier for twenty-two hours. That schedule ensured that every day would be a long day for Messcooks.

After eating a meal, the crew would place their trays into a scullery window and return to duty. Inside the window a Messcrank would dump the food left over into a trash can lined with a large plastic bag. The tray and utensils were put on a conveyor belt and moved to the dishwashers. When the bag in the trash can became full of food waste, it would be sealed as well as a person could expect it to be. Messcranking has certain dos and don'ts. Do take the garbage and regular trash out and throw it overboard on time. Do not make a mess of any other spaces when doing so. Do clean up any mess you make. Do not leave it for the owners of the space to clean.

The full bag of slop had to be carried to the fantail of the ship and tossed overboard. Getting it to the rear of the ship was sometimes tricky, at best. Messcooks took an established route from the messdecks to the fantail. Unfortunately, it required passing through the Marine Detachment (MarDet) area. The marines were berthed just below the fire deck, which served as a barrier between the hangar bay and the rest of the ship below. The fire deck is thick enough to impede a fire's progress to the lower levels of the ship. There was a hatch through which the garbage had to pass in order to make it to the hangar bay and the fantail. Since this hatch created a hole in the fire deck, the hatch had to be just as thick as the deck was. This thickness made the hatch heavier than most hatches, and that required a smaller opening to keep the hatch light enough to be closed quickly in case of a fire with minimal effort.

In order to dump garbage, a Messcook would climb two standard ladders up through two decks up to the MarDet compartment, transit that area to the hatch in the fire deck, and up onto the hangar bay. From there it was a fairly straight shot to the fantail. Getting a heavy plastic bag through this process is not easy. You have to carry the bag on your back like a seabag. When you come to the MarDet area, the hatch is smaller, and the bag will not fit through on your back. You cannot carry it in front of you because the ladder is steep, and it would be like hauling a nut-sac one hundred times bigger than you do naturally. So the best way is to step up the ladder backward and pull the slop bag after you.

Once in a while a bag would catch on something going through the fire deck hatch. It is a smaller opening with a hundred edges to catch clothing, skin, and slop bags. Once a bag is cut open, even slightly, the heavy load inside splits it wider fast, letting all the discarded food fly right out and onto the deck. It is bad enough that this happens at all and anywhere, but to have it occur in the MarDet is twice as bad. If the marines are not accompanying the skipper around, doing physical training, keeping their uniforms in order, or guarding the nuclear weapons locker, then they are keeping their area of the ship extremely polished and shiny.

Speaking of the nuclear weapons locker, at this point let me tell you that I can neither confirm nor deny the presence of nuclear weapons aboard any naval vessel.

So, when you break a bag of smelly food slop in the compartment owned by the marine detachment, you have just spit in their collective eyes. If this happens to you, it still has to be cleaned up no matter where it lands. If it happens in this area, then you have twenty or more marines yelling at you and monitoring your progress to return the area to its former shining glory. This actually happened to a couple of my friends. It was a horrible experience for them. I suppose they had nightmares for a while. Marines can be intimidating when they are in your face, and they know right is on their side.

My tour aboard the USS *Wasp* was over when it was decommissioned in July 1972. It had been a big learning experience for me. This was where I learned to work hard and to play hard. I was single, and my money was mine to do whatever I wanted with. Because I was too junior to have a car on base, even if I could have afforded one, the only entertainment to be had was at one of the clubs on base. I did my best to support the on-base clubs. It was the right thing to do, as I saw it.

On my first cruise aboard *Wasp* I was the only newbie in "E" Division. As the ship transited around Cape Hatteras, North Carolina, the sea became increasingly rougher. If you have ever made this transit you probably know exactly what I mean. The petty officers I worked for had me assist in burning out the windings of a motor in the Rewind Shop. The acrid smell along with other shipboard odors combined with the rolling and pitching deck to make me very uncomfortable stomach wise. That was what the POs wanted.

49

As I tried to ignore the feeling I was experiencing from the moving deck, they started to talk of greasy food and how seasick they had been once. Sure enough, in a short while, their hopes were realized . . . I was seasick. They had talked me into it. They were getting a big bang out of me, the just-out-of-boot-camp newbie, getting sick at sea. Without asking I jumped up and ran to the nearest head and started hugging a commode. I got there in the nick of time. As I cleaned myself up I noticed that a first class petty officer was wrapped around the commode next to mine.

No matter how long you serve in the navy, some days you get seasick, and some days you do not. I have been seasick on seas as smooth as glass. I have also been one of the few who could stand watch during a typhoon off the Philippines. For me the trigger is more a smell thing. As you walk from compartment to compartment on the ship the odors change depending on what is in that space. Firefighting foam is a trigger for me. Strangely enough, the smell of fuel makes me seasick. I spent my entire career in very close proximity with fuel oil. I worked in the propulsion engineering spaces on all my ships. Fuel makes me sick . . . go figure.

Before I left *Wasp* I participated in the advancement exam for third class petty officer. I somehow made the cutoff and was a third class when I transferred to my next command, USS *L. Y. Spear (AS-36)*, in Norfolk, Virginia.

Chapter 6

"Not another paint job!"

Much of my own leadership skills, or lack thereof, were developed over the years and influenced heavily by the Chiefs and Petty Officers who I had worked for. For their capable guidance I heartily thank them all. With few exceptions they always steered me in the right direction. I continue to have deep respect for the men and women in the chains of command that I have worked within over the years.

If you know me very well then you know I hate painting and the preparations it takes to ready the surface to be painted. I also hate yard work, but, again, a tale for the next book. My idea of Hell has to do with grinding down, preparing, and painting the decks in front of the switchboards located in the hot engineering spaces. This was one of my first jobs aboard the *Wasp*. "E" Division was in charge of the electrical switchboards in all the engineering spaces. Physical upkeep is a major part of that responsibility. Major electrical distribution switchboards can become very dangerous if not properly maintained.

Wasp was a World War II aircraft carrier commissioned November 24, 1943. The previous *Wasp* was *(CV-7)* and was lost in battle in 1942. The keel of *(CVS-18)* was originally laid down as USS *Oriskany* but quickly changed to *Wasp* to honor the loss of the last ship to bear that name. I think that some of the carriers of that era were built quickly and sent to war to satisfy the need in the fleet. No one was betting on whether they would survive and return.

Over the years the catwalk in front of the switchboard had been resurfaced many times. Sometimes while standing switchboard watches, I would look up into the corners of the space I was in and marvel at the cable runs that after thirty years appeared to have been just tossed up there. What were probably neat and orderly cable installations at commissioning had turned into a spaghetti-like mess caused by years of retrofits. A retrofit is the process of bringing a ship up to speed as far as the latest technology. Most of them require that new power cable runs be made to supply power to any new equipment. Due to the need for watertight integrity, cable runs must take certain routes. Looking at *Wasp* in my day you could see the helter-skelter way it all looked. The cables ran every which way with no rhyme or reason apparent. After years of constantly adding equipment, the cable runs look jumbled.

The deckplates went through the same retrofits as did the rest of the ship. My first deck was in Number Four Fireroom (FR4). It was typical of the rest. The space was very hot and humid; I come from Michigan and was not used to working in that type of climate. Wearing my work boots, dungarees, chambray shirt, T-shirt, respirator, hood, and ear protection, I spent day after day down there going from one switchboard to the next. Some of these deckplates had to be replaced totally.

By the time I was done, my working uniform looked like I had been in Deck Division for a while. No offense to anyone in the Deck Division, because they look the way they look due to the hard work they accomplish keeping the ship painted and looking good. Many guys in the Engineering Department look just as bad after doing the job that they do. My dungarees were stained with red lead primer and deck grey paint so badly that it was hard to tell that they were once the color of blue jeans. My boondockers were half-painted the same way, and the leather over the steel toes was ripped and starting to peel back. This has never been a look that I could personally appreciate. From day one in the navy, I always tried to keep my uniform in proper order.

Another aspect of the resurfacing job that made it difficult was the grinding of so much metal. The noise and dust from the deck were impossible to contain. It kept getting into your eyes, ears, and lungs. Plus the heat and the constant vibration seemed to never stop.

When the decks in front of the switchboards were finished, I silently rejoiced that the painting was over. Of course I was terribly wrong and premature in my personal celebration. In the US Navy the painting is never, ever done. The ships are constantly being painted from one end to the other, and when that is finished the whole thing is started again.

My leading petty officer, we all called him Woody for some reason, was there to inspect the finished product at the switchboard. He was also a petty officer I chose to emulate in my future career. I would not use the phrase "pleased with the job," but since he did not say anything negative, I suppose that was a major plus. At least he did not say something like, "Do it again." I was pleased with that.

"Well, I guess I'll take all this stuff back to the paint locker and turn it in," I just happened to say, and I started to gather all the equipment up.

"Take this stuff to the shop," he said. "Then go to the paint locker and get a five-gallon can each of red, white, and blue paint."

"Whoa," I thought, *"not another paint job!"*

"Oh, yeah," he said, giving me a challenging look. "You're painting the shop."

Sure enough, I painted the shop. This time I had help. Each switchboard had been assigned to a different fireman, and now that we were finished with them we could work as a team on our shop. The shop was clean and air-conditioned, and we could play our boom boxes as loud as we wanted. It was not as bad as in the fireroom, but it was still painting. The color scheme was to my liking too. When we finished, the shop was patriotically red, white, and blue. My favorite colors.

Chapter 7

"Someone has to stay and serve on the East Coast."

I was one of the last crewmen to leave USS *Wasp* in July 1972. My orders at that time were to report for duty aboard the *L. Y. Spear (AS-36)*, homeported in Norfolk, Virginia. These orders were different from my original set. When the detailer first handed out assignments I was being sent back to Newport, RI, and a ship homeported there. A friend of mine and I decided we wanted to go to Vietnam. So, we called the Detailer in Washington, DC, and asked for orders to "Nam." After a pause the Detailer said, "Listen to me, guys, someone has to stay and serve on the East Coast." He paused again. "Besides, one day you'll thank me for not sending you to Vietnam."

And I have secretly thanked him quite a few times in my career. I do not know what his name was or where he was from, but I have silently wished him and his family all the best. I added him to my "Thank God for Being There" list.

Even though we were not going to Vietnam, we still did not want to stay in Rhode Island either. I did not feel like I had left anything of value in Newport, so there was no reason for me to return there. One night we sat on the messdecks and tried to figure a way to change our orders. I wanted to go to Norfolk, Virginia, because my father lived in Clinton, Maryland, which is just outside the District of Columbia and within driving distance on the weekends. I cannot remember where my buddy wanted to go, but he wanted to leave Rhode Island.

By a quirk of fate the Electrical Officer (EO), a Lieutenant, happened to overhear our conversation. We never got very close to the EO. He was up the chain-of-command too far for us to see on a daily basis. To us he was just an old man with a commission and more power over us than we liked. He questioned us on the problem we had. This was not during working hours, but he still took the time to listen and come up with possible solutions. He listened, asked a few more questions, and told us to see him in the morning with a dream sheet filled out. A dream sheet is a form on which you let the detailer know your first three choices for location and command type for your next set of orders. Why is it called a dream sheet? Because it is a dream if you actually get what you put on that request. In reality, you go where the needs of the service send you. But, we were third classes and might fit into a lot of other billets. The more senior you become the fewer openings there are.

So, the next day we delivered our dream sheets to the Electrical Officer. He took them, and that was the last we heard from him on the subject. After a couple weeks, however, we both received new orders to the location we had requested. Now to be fair, I requested Norfolk, Virginia. Norfolk is home to the world's largest naval base. If they could not find a billet for an Electrician's Mate Third Class in that area somebody just was not looking. I do not remember where my friend requested to go. Well, as you can guess we were pretty darn happy with this turn of events. However, you just knew something would screw it all up.

What could possibly screw this transfer up? You can probably guess. The answer is a woman.

The occasion for my transfer was the decommissioning of the carrier. In July 1972 USS *Wasp (CVS-18)* was placed out of commission. I think they sold her for scrap. Hopefully, some of her ended up in another warship. During the months leading up to the end I was assigned to the crew closing it up. Most of the crew had already been transferred to other commands. Some of us in "E" Division decided to live off the ship. So we got together four or five guys and rented two apartments in an older home in Providence, Rhode Island. The house was on Peace Street. It was an older home that had been subdivided into three apartments. We rented two, and some civilians, poor souls, had the third. They turned out to be nice enough. We threw parties every day and got no complaints. I do not know how they put up with all our noise.

Our parties resulted in a couple walls of beer cans. We tried to build a wall with hard liquor bottles but, it just was not the same. I sure look proud of my wall.

One of my fellow sailors met a lady friend who lived in the area. She worked at the telephone company office in Pawtucket, RI. She happened to have some girlfriends, and she hooked up a few dates between them and our sailors. The parties just got bigger. Before you know it, spring had sprung, and there were marriages to be planned. So, everyone in the house was engaged to one of the local girls. Everyone, that is, except me. I had been spending my time at all the parties drinking. I guess I was the clown in the corner at all the shindigs. I enjoyed my corner, and no one else seemed to mind that I was quietly self-destructing over there. The ladies were concerned that my Bud(weiser) and I might be lonely. Well, you know women are not going to let that kind of stuff happen.

My buddies were still in that "give her what she wants" stage of their relationships. The women got the men together and hatched a plan. I was not privy to the plan, nor was I given the chance to bow out, which is what I would have done. They set me up with a blind date for one of the weddings. When the time came I went ahead, thinking to myself it is only one date. Was I in for a surprise! My date and her twin sister were cute. Identical twins (every man's dream, right?), who remind me of the set of twins on *The Simpsons* television show. Well, the master plan worked. We seemed to hit it off from the start. No more corner clown for me. It was love at first sight as far as I was concerned. In fact, as I write this some thirty-nine years later, it is still love at first sight. It is just a good thing that she really was blind (not really).

The only fly in the ointment came later, at the reception. I noticed that she had Band-Aids on her wrists. So, I just asked her what had happened. Cool as a cucumber and with a straight face she simply said, "I recently tried to commit suicide." Hold the phone! Now I am not usually that gullible, but she had said it so calmly. I might have even detected a strange, crazed look in her eyes. After some time she owned up to the fact it was just a joke. She had recently had an accident at home that had left the marks. I knew then that I had a girl with a sense of humor, a major plus to me. As thrilled as I was, the Electrical Officer on *Wasp* had a whole different take on the news.

There I was, falling in love with a girl from Rhode Island and I had transfer orders to Virginia. How is that for luck? Well, since it worked the last time, I went to the Electrical Officer for help in getting my orders switched back to Newport so I could be close to Donna, the girl I loved. I cannot remember if it was what he said or what he did not say that clued me in to the fact that he was not doing anything with my orders again. He was somewhat vocal in his displeasure. What follows is the clean part.

"I spent three hours on the phone last time to get them changed to Norfolk." He seemed on the verge of a stroke. Is the word I am looking for *apoplectic?*

"There is no way I'm going to do that again," he said firmly. "No way, no way!"

The rest is history. Love be damned, I spent my next tour of duty on a submarine tender in Norfolk, Virginia. But the young lady and I have managed to stay together for almost forty years, including the time period we dated long distance. When it was all over, about five couples from the group ended up getting married. I know of two couples whose marriages did not last, one of them being the wedding where we met. Unfortunately, another couple was killed together in a traffic accident, having been married over thirty years. They were good friends and a great match for each other.

My tour on *Wasp* was my first attached to a ship. It was my first sea duty. I guess in a way it will always be my favorite. I had a lot of fun and no responsibility. It was that period of time when there was no way that I would ever reenlist. There was only one major cruise, and that was to the Mediterranean Sea. We spent some time in the rough and very cold North Atlantic during another cruise. Discussion on those events will wait for the next book. I made Petty Officer Third Class before I left *Wasp* to go to my next command. That promotion would change the way I approached the rest of my career. I reported to the next ship already a petty officer so I felt a bit surer of myself. Automatically, I received a measure of authority that I had never felt before. There is always a different feeling between shipmates who witness your promotion and those who meet you for the first time after you are wearing the new stripes. It can feel personally rewarding to say, "I am a Petty Officer." Slowly my attitude was evolving toward a career mind-set. I never saw it coming.

Chapter 8

"Bishop, canary suit, pronto!"

I took two weeks of leave between *Wasp* and *L. Y. Spear*. It is common practice for navy personnel to take a couple weeks between commands. Of course, you should have leave time on the books so there is no danger of going into the hole as far as vacation time. I spent the better part of July 1972 visiting my family, and at one point was able to introduce my future wife, Donna, to my father.

The first thing I did was to take Donna to Washington, DC, to meet my father and stepmother. We spent a few days there and had a good time. After she returned home to Rhode Island, I went home to Pinckney. The month of July has decent weather in Michigan, so I spent that time with my mother and brothers. We fished, swam, and basically relaxed. I had the most fun because they all had jobs to go to every day. For some reason when the time came for me to return, I was ready to get to my next ship. I was starting to like serving on active duty. The navy was slowly becoming a life for me.

Getting away from the US Navy for a couple of weeks is a necessity. The downtime is great for recharging your batteries in preparation for a new duty station. When you check aboard a new command they expect you to hit the deck running and start easing the workload on the existing crew.

The USS *L. Y. Spear* (AS-36) was a submarine tender, or repair ship. Tenders supply needed services to any ship that wishes to receive them. Those services include water, sewage, phone, and electrical power, among others. A tender is a floating repair shop and fabrication factory. Onboard are complete machine shops, refrigeration and air-conditioning shops, welder and fitter shops, and electrical shops. *L. Y. Spear* even had unique shops just for submarines, such as the periscope shop. I was stunned the first time I saw a periscope out of the boat and lying on a bench in the shop. I never would have guessed how long and how big they are. If the tender cannot provide it or make it, then you do not need it.

The ship was berthed at the Destroyer and Submarine Piers (D&S Piers) in Norfolk, Virginia. At that time the D&S Piers were physically separate from the main base. There were always nuclear and diesel subs floating in and out of this area, and most of the time at least one was tied outboard *Spear*. I cannot tell anything about the boats. Not because I am sworn to secrecy or held by some ancient oath, but because I do not know anything about those boats except that when they required power we supplied it to them. What they did with it once they got it is a mystery to me.

Because there was the possibility of an accident that might cause some type of contamination, every day the duty section ran practice drills on how to react in such an emergency. I absolutely hated these drills. I know they were necessary, and I know that if it ever came to it I would be glad for the top-notch training we got. But, I hated donning those damn canary suits. Each day when the team mustered, two or three guys were chosen to wear the bright yellow suits.

It was like being back in high school, and the teacher was picking a student to read his or her paper out loud to the class. The teacher stands at the head of the classroom and looks at the sea of faces to determine who gets to read his or her paper. Do you look enthusiastic and really prepared? Do you try to not make eye contact with the teacher because she will call on you to read? Or do you throw up in the aisle between the rows of desks and feign illness? I learned in middle school that the throw-up thing does not really work. What I used to do is just sit there on the deck by the damage control locker with my attention on my boondockers, my work boots, and hope someone else got called. Of course I was just a dumb third class petty officer and did not realize that the Senior Chief in charge of the Damage Control Team used a list to ensure all team members got the opportunity to play canary. When my name came up on his list I heard, "Bishop, canary suit, pronto!"

Long-sleeved shirt buttoned at the neck and wrist, pant legs tucked into your socks, hat fully covering your head. On top of that layer of clothing you put on a one-piece canary yellow hazmat suit, heavy rubber boots, and a gas mask over your face. That should cover as much of your head as possible and anything not covered by the suit's hood. These drills last from forty-five minutes to an hour, or until everybody gets it right. That whole time you are standing in a passageway just above the engineering spaces, and you are sweating your *gonads off!* If the drill requires that you go into one of the spaces, then the temperature gets far worse. Luckily, if I remember, we were on six section duty. I only had to worry about the suit once every six days, and then only if my name came up on the list that Senior Chief used.

The tour aboard *Spear* was not as eventful as some of the others were. But, it was where I came up with a short little ditty with a theme that ran true throughout the years I was on active duty. It goes like this:

"Onboard, on duty; Out of sight, out of mind; Off the ship, hard to find."

If you live aboard the ship you are most likely to be pulled from your bunk in the middle of the night if something goes wrong, whether or not you have duty that night. Since the *L. Y. Spear* was a tender, work was in progress 24/7.

One cold, rainy winter night it was so windy that the ship was being pushed away from the pier. The *Spear* was constantly tied to Pier 22 in the D&S Pier section of the Norfolk Naval Base. As a tender, it had to be available when a submarine needed repairs. This meant that the ship spent most of its time in port. Shore power was hardly ever disconnected from a tender. On this stormy night the wind was blowing the 644-foot-long vessel away from and then back against the pier. *L. Y. Spear* had a displacement of 22,640 tons. This was no small ship. The continuous movement of the ship caused the shore power cables to pull out away from the pier. When the wind returned the ship to the pier again, the stretched-out cables sagged enough to get them trapped between the ship and the pier.

I happened to be the Duty Electrician that night. I was called out and had to get the others in the duty section from "E" Division so we could fix the situation. It was still early in the morning, so we went on ship's power using the emergency generator. Our next job was to stay on the pier in the weather and try to pull the cables back up onto the pier when the ship moved away again. By now the weather had begun to deteriorate even more. The rain had turned to a mist and was starting to freeze to everything it touched. The four of us were so bundled up that we had a hard time moving around.

We spent about three hours outside on the pier trying to pull up the cables. Our cold fatigue got to us, and we even started pushing against the ship in an effort to physically move it. If you refer to the length and displacement figures above you will see the futility of such an act. There we were, literally leaning against the side of the ship with our shoulders and pushing with our feet against the pier. Can you imagine four sailors trying to push a ship of that size, or any size, away from the pier? That is how cold, hungry, and tired we were that night.

As the crew returned in the morning to start the day, and the senior personnel surveyed the situation, it was decided to have tugboats give us a hand. If I remember right, the four of us had made that suggestion hours earlier. But, so-and-so was a Commander or Captain and could see that tugs were needed. What were we, chopped liver? At daybreak the cables had been returned to where they were supposed to be with no damage to the ship or crew, and any damaged cables were replaced . . . by the new duty section.

Chapter 9

"I could snap your neck . . . no one could stop me!"

One of the things you look forward to while serving in the navy is a periodic shore duty tour. After being on sea duty for five to six years, your batteries really need to be recharged. As an Electrician's Mate my sea/shore rotation was six/two. As a Gas Turbine Specialist it was six/two. The constant grind of sea duty takes its toll on every crew member. Each ship goes through a cycle of readiness inspections and exams over a designated period of time. Some of these evolutions can be grueling and leave you pretty exhausted. Every department on the ship has its own specialized series of major examinations.

In the Engineering Department, the department I spent my career in, the Operational Propulsion Plant Examination (OPPE) is the test that can make or break a ship and the crew. I cannot overstate the stress levels that these requirements put on the men who keep the ship functioning as it must. When one thing is completed, the ship heads right into another test and then another until the cycle starts over again. Most ships are in a constant high tempo of operations. Shore duty is the only respite personnel get.

My first shore duty command, from November 1973 to November 1975, was at the Naval Photographic Center (NPC) in Washington, DC. Some have described it as "Hollywood on the Potomac." It is now known as the Naval Imaging Command. NPC is located on Anacostia Naval Annex at one end of Bolling Air Force Base. The time I spent there was very enjoyable.

This was, after all, the time period when I got married to Donna, and she relocated from Rhode Island to Maryland and moved in with me. We were married on Saturday, November 2, 1974. We lived in a one-bedroom apartment in Suitland, Maryland, just outside the District's border. We also lived about five miles from where my father lived. It was nice having family around.

Since I was an Electrician's Mate Second Class (EM2) and not a Photographer's Mate (PM), my billet was in the First Lieutenant's Office (1st Lt's). The First Lieutenant's office on ship was Deck Department. At NPC we took care of all building and grounds maintenance associated with the command. It was a tour perfect for recharging your batteries. As an added bonus, we shared the parking lot with the Six-Five-Four Club, catering to the Non-Commissioned Officers. My office being too close to a base club or a package store, the base liquor store, caused a number of personal problems for me.

Though it was officially an enlisted club for military Noncoms, E-4 through E-6, service members of all ranks and branches frequented this lively watering hole. The club served drinks and food starting at lunch and continuing to closing. It was very convenient having the club about fifteen yards from our office. Our wives would attest to the fact that it was a little more than convenient; it was way too close. If the first lieutenant's crew missed a lunch at the club, it was through no fault of our own.

The division consisted of a Lieutenant, a Chief Petty Officer, myself and one other EM2, and the rest of the men, who numbered around fifteen to twenty at any given time. It was a pretty mixed group. The Lieutenant was a navy pilot by occupation. The Chief, an EMC, came to us from the world of submarines. A Hull Technician First Class (HT1), the other EM2, and I were all from the surface fleet. The rest were from the Photographer Mate's (PH) world.

Since NPC was the capital of the PH world, and since it did not have a galley to messcook in, the junior personnel did a stint in the First Lieutenant's department. We worked on everything from building electrical work to replacing walls. Lest my brother, who is an electrician in the real world, have a heart attack, let me say that our electrical work was accomplished under the watchful gaze of a licensed civilian electrician. I add that statement because he has seen my electrical work at home.

When a job got to be too big for the manpower we had, or if for some reason we needed additional people, we could always draw from the disciplinary hold personnel. These sailors and marines were waiting for captain's mast or courts-martial for various crimes. Some of their violations were serious in nature, but if they were deemed nonviolent and not a flight risk, they could be sent on working parties.

During the early years of the Cold War, government buildings were used to store supplies in case an emergency developed. Years before I was stationed there, the crawl space beneath the Photo Center was used to store fresh water. I do not remember the exact count, but there must have been three hundred or more thirty-gallon barrels of water below the building. These drums had been lined with thick heavy-plastic bladders that held the water secured against contamination and prevented rusting of the containers. A thirty-gallon metal barrel of water is very heavy and awkward to maneuver. I referred to the area under the building as a crawl space because there were only a few spots where you could stand up.

The Potomac River is a stone's throw away from the Photo Center and the water table is just below the surface. Sometimes heavy rains would result in a flooded parking lot. Water backing up in the parking lot did not deter any of us from the Six-Five-Four Club, however. There was no basement to speak of, so no one noticed all the water that the barrels rested in. Of course eventually they did notice the problem and called a working party to take care of it.

Since a petty officer second or above had to be in charge of the disciplinary hold guys, those of us meeting that criterion met to decide who would have to take it. Well, the Lieutenant was not even considered. If you know anything about the navy, you know that the Chief was only in the meeting to ensure the decision was made fairly and above reproach. It did not take me long to see where this was going. The HT1, the other EM2, and I voted on the outcome. By a vote of two to one it was decided that the junior petty officer present should take charge of the working party. That would not be the only time in my career that I took it in the shorts because I was junior.

My fellow petty officers were actually looking out for me. They wanted me to get experience in leading troops, even if those troops were dangerous felons. Boy, my shipmates, you just have to admire them. They were keeping my best interests at heart. The fact that the job did not start until after lunch had nothing to do with the decision. After lunch at the club, who would feel like working?

The working party arrived on time right after lunch. There were five or six of them, and they all looked to me like they would bolt for freedom at any second. I took muster, and we started to work. Believe me, it was a ball-busting job. Each barrel had to be manhandled from the deep recesses of the crawl space. The space had the appearance of catacombs, only without all the headroom. Everybody had clean, neat, working uniforms when we started, but within a few minutes we looked as though we had been living in the muddy underworld. I am trying to convey the crappy conditions under NPC that we were working in. Only the dog-sized rats down there could enjoy the atmosphere. The rats contributed to the scene by dropping human-sized feces. I hated stepping in that shit.

The job was finished in about a week. After the first day, we worked both morning and afternoon. Every day we got more men from the disciplinary barracks. One or two of them were there the whole time, but some were rotated in and out. During our breaks we generally sat in the back of one of the pickup trucks and shot the bull, navy style. That means we talked about girls, booze, girls, booze, and life as a whole. In the middle of one of the lunch breaks the conversation went toward what the guys had done to end up in the Disciplinary Unit. There were the usual problems of AWOL, assault, and theft crimes that you would expect. But, one day, the big guy sitting in the bed of the truck and leaning against the back of the cab had a story to tell of his own. Beware of the quiet one in the corner; he has secrets to tell.

"I'm waiting here for attempted rape and assault with intent to kill." He was very calm when he said it. All his comrades seemed to acknowledge what he was saying. This definitely got my attention. To this day I do not know whether to believe his claim or not. I would like to think that the people in charge would not put someone with that serious a crime on a general working party. But, who really knows for sure?

"Did you do it?" I asked him.

"Yeah." Still as calm as before he added, "It was an officer's daughter." He paused—for effect, I guess. "Ya know that crow on your arm don't mean anything to me. I could snap your neck right now, and no one could stop me." I think he was big enough to do just that too.

At that time, right there, I felt that he was definitely telling the truth. It made the rest of the day very long. That was his only day there. He never came to work with us again. I do not remember why he did not come back, but I know he never did. That was fine by me.

The EMC(SS) we worked for at the time did me a great service that took years for me to appreciate. I really did not want to do it, but he made me write evaluations for the personnel junior to me. Until that point I had not had to do any real paperwork. I was getting fat, dumb, and happy without touching paper. I guess he saw that I had already reenlisted once and would probably make it a career.

So, as much as I did not like it, he was getting me prepared for the future. It paid off in dividends later in my professional life. I once had a Main Propulsion Assistant (MPA) who told me how much he appreciated the way I wrote evaluations because most of the department Chiefs turned them in written in Crayola. The MPA is second in the chain of command in the ship's Engineering Department.

The Six-Five-Four Club was as popular to personnel outside of the navy as it was to us. A lot of air force men and women came from their club on Bolling Air Base after getting a buzz. I always thought that they got going in the Air Force Club and came to the Navy Club to get rowdy. In the evening the club was pretty crowded. I know this because I was there most nights. We even had men coming from the Soldiers and Sailors Home.

One older retired marine used to have a taxi drop him off and pick him up at the same times every day. He only drank two or three beers and then left. Every time he finished a beer he would say in a very loud voice, "One dead soldier!" and then toss the empty beer can back over his head. People sitting behind him were used to this, and the minute his voice raised they took shelter from the flying can. Sometimes I think he used to smash the can on his forehead before launching it. Were there aluminum cans then? He was just one of the more colorful people to populate this watering hole.

Chapter 10

"Hey, I stepped on his Corfams!"

From March 1976 to March 1977 I was stationed aboard the USS *La Salle (AGF-3)*, homeported in Manama, Bahrain, a small island nation in the Persian Gulf. The time I was there was different from what the present-day Middle East is. The Shah of Iran was still in power, and most people in America had no idea what a Bahrain was, let alone where it was located. I was there before the Mid-East was fashionable. It was during this tour that I was advanced to First Class Electrician's Mate, on July 16, 1976.

One of the missions that the ship was engaged in was showing the flag of the United States around that area of the globe. USS *La Salle* was flagship for Commander Middle East Force, who from June 1976 through the end of my tour and beyond was Admiral William J. Crowe, the future Chairman of the Joint Chiefs of Staff. From my experience, Admiral Crowe was a very approachable man.

We did not put the ship on shore power very often. Shore power was not always available in Bahrain. When the opportunity presented itself, we did so gladly. Rigging shore power was one of the first things I learned when I went to my first ship. I learned how heavy those damn cables were, and how hard to maneuver and contrary they can be, especially in inclement weather. The cables weigh a ton, it seems, when you have to hump them up and down ladders, the side of the ship, or over and around deck machinery. It is also very dangerous, like many evolutions aboard ship, if the crew is not paying attention to what they are doing.

You are always undermanned when pulling shore cables. Shipmates just somehow get lost or do not hear the call for shore power to be rigged. It usually gets accomplished before liberty call for the ship electricians. Believe me when I say that there were plenty of times when I felt like not showing up to run those stupid cables. But being on shore power meant fewer watchstanders and more guys on liberty.

One summer day on *La Salle* we were having a tough time with the big extension cords (shore power cables). It was really hot, and tempers were flaring. Again we were undermanned and had to pull cables on the ship, then go to the pier and pull the cables there, and return to the ship to repeat the process. This was going to go on until all three cables were onboard and in position. I felt as if we were only inching the cables into place. At one point we were on the ship, and I was last man on the cable.

It was the same as playing tug-of-war, only the cables were winning. Being the last man on the line meant that I was holding the cable in front of me up and pulling, but the cable behind me had no one to support it, and it dropped quickly to the deck after it had gone through my arms. That added weight made it very hard to pull from the front of the line while pushing the cable behind me. I was assisted by another crewman, who happened by and decided to help. I could have made it through, but the help was greatly appreciated. Imagine my surprise when I turned to say thanks and found out it was Admiral Crowe, and he was still holding his section of cable.

"Where do you want me to put this now?" Words any sailor likes to hear. But not coming from an Admiral. That is especially true when the first answer that popped into my dirty mind was not an answer that I could get away with saying to an Admiral. I cleared my thoughts and went on.

I cannot swear to it, but I think the first words actually out of my mouth were something like, "abba, abba, abba . . ." While I am stuttering, he is looking as though he would really like to get rid of this weight he is holding. Luckily for me it was almost in position already. "Ah, just drop it there, Admiral, th-that'd be great."

"Whew, it's hot, huh?"

"Yes, sir, it sure is." Almost as an afterthought I said, "Listen, Sir, we really appreciate your help, but we'd have got it."

"Yes, I know. You guys have a good day," he said, and he left.

I had seen the Admiral prior to that but never in that type of situation. Over the course of my career I have witnessed many occurrences of officers forgetting their commissions and working like one of the men, especially in the Engineering Department. Probably more times than not they pitched in and helped, but no one ever forgot who was who in the chain of command. Speaking of the chain of command, I used to try figuring out how many people would have to die in the chain before I became President. There would be way too many for me, but it was a thought. If that ever happened, there would not be much left to be President of. Of course, if that were the case, there would not be much for me to screw up, either.

Many Americans think that the Middle East is always hot. The winter months can get cold and nasty. On *La Salle* we shifted to the winter uniform on time with the rest of the navy. So, it was on a winter day on an upper deck that I had another encounter with the Admiral. I was up on the same deck where the shore power cables were connected. We were working in the afternoon, and another US Navy ship was coming alongside to moor. No one on my working party was paying attention until we heard the word passed to "brace for collision!" That got our attention, especially since we were tied to the pier.

An example of a Captain's Gig. This is not the one damaged on *LaSalle*.

The ship coming alongside was coming too fast, and the two vessels collided. The only damage I can remember was to the Captain's Gig. When I heard the word passed I immediately shifted my weight to my right foot and started to go to the left to run over and see what had happened. As I did this my first step put my left foot on top of a crewman's right shoe. We bumped each other slightly, and I lightly started to move him out of my way. I was looking down and could only see our feet.

It was just dawning on me that the other guy was wearing Corfams when I saw his right sleeve slide into my view. All I could see was his ranking on the end of his dress coat sleeve. I had never been that close to that much gold in my life. I snapped to attention and started to apologize for stepping on his foot and gouging his Corfam shoe. Corfams are those shiny and expensive shoes that many of the navy's khaki-clad community wear with their dress uniform.

"Excuse me, Admiral, I . . ."

The Admiral was more worried about the two ships and any damage to them. I do not think he even looked at me. He eased me aside and went to the side to view the accident, saying something like, "Ah, yeah . . ."

I never heard about the incident again. But later, when he was the Chairman of the Joint Chiefs and I saw him on television I would mention to anyone who would listen, "Hey, I stepped on his Corfams." And I smiled a big grin.

Some things are looked upon with great fear by most sailors. At the top of the list is a shipboard fire, especially at sea, and man overboard. Both are taken very seriously by all parties. There are constant drills to keep the ship's crew in top form for recovering from these crises. Officers of the Deck (OOD), Helmsmen, and the entire bridge crew are well trained in recovery of men overboard. Likewise, those in the engineering spaces are trained to fight fires as first respondents until the fire teams get there.

On *La Salle* there was a television station that showed movies and TV shows sent to us by Armed Forces Radio and Television System (AFRTS—pronounced A-FARTS). I think that it goes by another name currently. I was friends with the Interior Communications First Class Petty Officer (IC1) who ran the facility and spent some time up there where it was quiet. It was during one of these visits that a man went over the side. As soon as the alarm goes off everybody reports to a predetermined space for a muster. That is where they identify the missing sailor when he does not show to be counted. Our muster was in "E" Division berthing, and everyone onboard the ship was listed as present and accounted for. After two or three musters with no one missing they let us know that it was a drill. No one had gone over. But, had this been a real man overboard, the muster would have been wrong. Someone would still be floating out there all by himself. Since the muster is so vital and a life hangs in the balance, the LPO who takes and signs the faulty muster should be ready for the shit to hit the fan. Unfortunately, this time it was me.

You cannot believe how it feels to submit a muster in error and think that because of you a man might be floating in the ocean. No matter what actions are taken on you, think of him out there by himself.

The "E" Division Officer (DIVO) came looking for me right after the drill was secured. At least he was not the rant-and-rave type. There was an excellent reason why I turned in a bad muster report. The man overboard was the IC1 who I was talking to when the alarm sounded. I saw him, and there was no reason for him to leave the AFRTS studio. But when a drill is initiated, someone, in this case the Executive Officer (XO), has to pick a crew member and hide him to test the mustering procedures. After I left the IC1, the XO came by and grabbed him to be the man overboard. In the future I believe they hid a man prior to calling man overboard.

Sometimes they use "Oscar" as the man over the side. Oscar is a dummy made up of material wearing a life jacket that they toss into the sea. The hope is that someone along the sides of the ship will see the human form float by and report it. I only remember one man going over the side. The ship was in the North Atlantic, which is known for being very cold and rough. As I remember it, he was never recovered.

Men have gone over the side in port too. A ship had been listing one of its crew as Absent Without Leave (AWOL) for a couple weeks. He was a good sailor and everybody was confused as to why he would go missing. Ships are moved around in port for a number of reasons. This ship was moved or got under way or for some reason left its berth. Another ship was moved into that spot. The next day the second ship found a body floating beside it. It was the missing man. He had evidently stumbled off the gangway, and no one noticed. So for two weeks his body was trapped down there, and when the ships moved, the activity broke the body loose, and it came to the surface overnight.

A horrifying incident happened during a refueling evolution one day that exemplifies just how dangerous at-sea duty can become. The US Navy refuels on the go. The fueling ship rides beside the vessel taking on fuel, and in this way little time is lost in moving toward a commitment. I understand that the Soviet Navy could not master this feat until sometime in the late 1970s.

Apparently they refueled their ships at anchor. Think of the lost time doing it that way.

Running together at close quarters is extremely dangerous. The bridge crew and the deck crew are all well trained to do their jobs. They have to monitor things I cannot even think of. I was lucky in that I was always below deck in the engineering spaces during these evolutions. Underway Replenishments (Un-Reps) were done at any time of the day or night and in any type of weather. In the event of a national emergency we could not wait to take on supplies until the conditions were nicer.

While running alongside an oiler one day, our crew noticed a rogue wave wash high on the oiler's side and pull one of its crew over the railing and onto the main deck below. He appeared to be unconscious and was rolling around the deck. It is a scary situation seeing a sailor on the other ship that close to going over. They failed to notice for a few precious seconds and almost did not get to him in time. Luckily, King Neptune did not want that sailor on that day. He was successfully rescued and taken to sick bay.

Chapter 11

"Bees? You've got to be kidding me. How big are they?"

Sri Lanka is an island nation located in the Indian Ocean immediately south of the Indian subcontinent. In recent years the country has been the site of major unrest and rebellion. That was not the case in the summer of 1976 when the USS *La Salle* pulled into Colombo, the nation's capital. The ship was there for a few days of showing the flag and for some rest and relaxation for the crew. Usually when a ship hits a foreign port the local vendors descend upon the vessel plying their wares, sometimes setting up shop on the messdecks. They sell anything from small, cheap trinkets to wood carvings on up to ivory statues.

The statues were always interesting to me. You could tell that the same individual carved them all. They were exactly alike even down to the bubble in the bottom. Of course, real ivory does not have bubbles in the surface. These statues were not ivory but some material that had been molded into various shapes. The mold put a little bubble in the bottom of each one in exactly the same way. Still, the fake ivory statues did seem to sell. When you are overseas it is buyer beware.

I had not planned to go anywhere off the ship in this port but was looking forward to a relaxing couple of days. When the vendors were done selling on the messdecks and started to pack up, one went over to the Interior Communications First Class I mentioned in a previous chapter. The Sri Lankan had one more thing to sell. He had worked out an overnight tour for four or five sailors to

76

go on. IC1 thought it was a good deal, so he got a few shipmates together and signed on. They came and got me because they needed one more guy. I have always liked tours, and since this was going to be off the beaten path, I decided to join the group. It would turn out to be one of the most exhilarating experiences of my life.

In the middle of Sri Lanka's jungle is a humongous rock jutting out of the treetops. The Sigiriya Rock has been used for many things over the centuries, and now it is a tourist mecca. It stands over twelve thousand feet above sea level, and the sides are just cliff faces that drop hundreds of feet straight down. At the top of the rock are the ruins of a once-great palace. Getting from the bottom to the top to see the ruins was very treacherous. Today there are steps and catwalks for the interested tourist to ascend to the top. When our tour group arrived there was precious little to grab onto in case of an emergency. The crowds of visitors to the rock were not as great then as they are now. I can remember one or two people walking around. They were probably wondering if the climb was worth it.

Sri Lankan countryside seen from halfway up the Sigiriya Rock.

Our tour group was crazy enough to go wherever the guide took us. We saw the rock on the second day of the trip. The first day was short because of the arrival duties we had and just barely getting started before nightfall. Day one had its own rewards, however, and we spent the night in a hotel like something out of a Hollywood movie. If John Wayne had shown up it would have been *Hatari* all over again. For those of you too young to remember, John "The Duke" Wayne was an actor, and *Hatari* was one of his movies. I guess in my sixties I feel like some things need to be explained more thoroughly.

The safari-looking hotel was the real item. There was an open courtyard in the center with a large table for the dining guests; name an animal from the area and you would find its head on the wall somewhere. We each had our own room, complete with private toilet and shower. It was more private than the toilet in boot camp, anyway. The big mosquito net around the bed gave it an authenticity that had to be seen to appreciate.

When I asked how big the mosquitoes were around there, our guide laughed and said, "No mosquitoes." And then, like he was searching for the right word, "Bats!"

"Bats?"

"Yes, big bats fly here." I was not all that amused, but he apparently was.

"Okay," I said as I looked closer at the net and realized how strong it was. I felt a little safer, but I still was not laughing.

Food and an after-dinner walk took up the rest of the evening. The walk provided a moment of concern when we found ourselves being challenged by a wild boar. The guide had not wanted us to go for a walk, but we had insisted and now we could see why he was against the idea. I cannot think of anything boars are afraid of, and I suspect that if there were a list, American sailors would not be on it. Our guide made some noise and got in front of us while motioning us to back off the way we had come. Suddenly being in a listening mood, we followed his directions. The boar must have decided that the dead meat he had in his possession was worth more than chasing us would yield. After he snorted a couple times he ran off into the jungle. We stayed on the road with the guide and returned to the hotel.

The next morning we got up early and had coffee, fresh fruit, and biscuits. Like the evening meal, the breakfast was excellent. We rode in the car for a while and parked it to hike the rest of the way. The Sigiriya Rock is much more impressive in person than any picture can make it. The story given to us by our guide was that way back in history this palace was successfully defended by about five thousand men against approximately thirty thousand opposing troops below. A lot of the foundation still exists up there. In order to see what is left of the palace you must climb up to the top.

This involved a rusty stairway, rickety catwalks with no railings, and shallow footholds cut into the rock by some ancient resident for your hands and feet. We climbed to the top and got an outstanding view of the valley. It was not hard to believe that an outnumbered force could hold their own on top of a perch like this. Early people had dug wells for water in a few spots so the army would not go without water. Those wells were still wet when we were there.

In 1977 there was a spot toward the top where no catwalk or stairway existed. Only a few bars were sticking out about every ten feet that you could grab to steady yourself. We actually had to use the original hand and foot holds to progress any farther. Looking down from that point truly made you feel like you were sitting on top of the world. One tiny misstep would plunge one or more of us hundreds of feet to the valley below.

The fear and the adventure were exhilarating to me. It was an experience I will never forget. When I think about it now I realize how crazy we were to climb up there. But we were young and dumb and full of piss and vinegar.

On the way back down we passed through an area of the path that I had noticed on the way up. About ten to fifteen feet of the path was covered by what we call "chicken wire."

"What's the chicken wire for?" I inquired.

"Bees," was the guide's reply. I started to think of how large a bee would have to become before chicken wire kept him out.

"Bees? You've got to be kidding me. How big are they?"

He held up one hand in the shape of a fist as if to demonstrate the size. Then he pointed to the side of the cliff. What I had earlier taken for a large growth of moss or some type of vine blowing back and forth in the wind was really a hell of a lot of big, hovering bees. Fortunately, our path took us nowhere near the bees.

The easiest way to see it now is through the *National Geographic Magazine*. They have some great pictures of the Sigiriya Rock and an article about the bees.

The rest of that day was spent seeing some of the sights that tourists usually visited. One of my friends got to ride, or sit upon, an elephant. Between the bats, the boar, and the bees we were all ready to get back to our own slice of America, the USS *LaSalle*.

Chapter 12

"I think we should get out of here, tho'."

As with anything else, there were some not-so-nice moments in my navy career. I intentionally left out the bad times because I wanted this to be an enjoyable read. However, a couple of things happened during our visits to Karachi, Pakistan, that I feel will illuminate the difference between our own culture and that of other, poorer nations. On my first visit to Karachi I saw the incredibly crowded streets. The roads were too packed for sardines. With the crowds there were the usual pickpockets and beggars, a staple of all countries on the planet.

Pakistani street scene.

The beggar who I remember most vividly was a woman with her two sons lying on a holey blanket along the curb, just barely off the street. She was clearly in the grip of some disease that turned her joints into twisted knots of useless flesh. Her knees and elbows were horrifyingly misshapen and probably were not very useful to her. I am not attempting to be colorful here. Her jaw appeared to be disjointed, and one eye was clouded over.

The first son was covered with sores that made my own psoriasis seem somewhat tame by comparison. He held out his hand and grinned widely. His ulcer-covered face would have been received better if he had had no teeth, instead of the hideous ones he displayed. I am not a physician, and I know that some things can be faked. I know that in foreign countries Americans are preyed upon by hustlers claiming their need for money to help some sickness, somewhere. With these two I may have been duped. I doubt that, but who really knows for sure?

The second son was for real. He sat on the blanket resting his body weight on an outstretched arm and hand. Opposite that arm were both his legs, bent at the knee. His free arm was used in the begging endeavor. He also had many sores on his body. The most striking difference between this one and his mother and brother was a very serious infection in his legs that oozed pus and gave off a very repulsive smell. He only had one foot. The other foot looked as though it had been sliced off with a meat slicer, as though someone had started just below his knee and sliced at an angle so that the blade finished cutting through an inch before the ankle. Given the sights, sounds, and smells, this was one of my worst liberty calls.

All that remained of that leg was rotting flesh and bone opened to the world. His grin was as hideous as his brother's. The world walked around these three and left them to suffer. The streets of Karachi were full of such scenes. On a subsequent visit I saw just the mother and brother. I pointed to the empty space on the blanket and asked where he was. We did not speak the same language, but her gestures were plain enough. The second son was gone.

On another visit to Pakistan a few friends and I got a four-wheeled carriage to take us where we wanted to go. Taxis in Karachi were dangerous, and they smelled inside. I guess our American sensitivities could not handle the stench that the Karachi population "enjoyed" every day. The carriage was slower, but it was nicer out in the air even with the smells.

As slow as the ride was, the most incredible thing happened. The driver apparently did not see a man on a bicycle who started in front of him. Before anyone could yell out, the front axle and both wheels crossed over the man and his bicycle, and we felt a big bump. He was lying in the street between the front and rear axles. Without skipping a beat the carriage driver backed up and again traveled over the man in the street; we felt another bump and the whole situation was starting to make us wonder.

"We hired him. Are we responsible?" I asked a buddy.

"I have no idea," he said. "I think we should get out of here, tho'."

Before we could react, the bicyclist slowly stood up halfway and dragged his bike and himself to the side of the road, where he collapsed. When he cleared the front of the carriage, the driver immediately continued down the street. To our knowledge, no one in the immediate area came to the rescue of the man with the bike. We have always heard that in many countries the fare is responsible for any accident the driver is involved in. For a split second there, we saw our lives tumbling out of control. I am sure that I would not like a Pakistani prison, but I was young then, and they might have liked me (ha-ha).

So the four of us just kept quiet and waited until we reached our destination, the International Hotel. When we arrived we could not get out of the carriage fast enough. Nothing ever came out of this accident, much to our relief. It shows how the many cultures making up the planet are very diverse. Life in Karachi is cheap and fragile. There were other incidents throughout my career, but these have stuck out from the rest. These have left vivid images in my mind.

There were a lot of craftsmen in the city of Karachi. I bought a few jewelry boxes for my wife and other relatives. The young man I bought them from tapped strips of brass into the lid in the shape of my wife's name and that of the other recipients, in cursive. You could also find a lot of marble in various shapes, such as glasses, card holders, cigarette holders, and more. Those who were interested could also find the drugs they wanted.

Karachi was one of the easiest places to buy illegal drugs that I can remember in my career. A quick disclaimer here, I do not now nor have I ever taken unsanctioned or nonprescription pharmaceuticals. I have enough bad habits without doing that stuff. I used to tell everyone that I would turn in my own mother if I found her with drugs. That kept guys from hanging around me if there were drugs on their person. A real shipmate would not put you in a position where you would have to decide whether to turn him in for drug possession or possibly be arrested with him for guilt by association.

When coming back from liberty to the ship all crewmen were searched. Quite a few bought souvenir camel saddles. They were really replicas made to be used as footstools in the living room. They were nice enough souvenirs, but I never bought one. A lot of guys tried to smuggle their drugs on board by sewing them inside the camel saddles. Usually the stitching was obvious to even the most untrained eye, so many of them got caught. Every camel saddle that came on board was thoroughly searched, and only fools would try that trick.

This was 1976 and, as a First Class Petty Officer, I was assigned to assist in searching the crew as they returned. While searching one guy I found drugs in his sock, but as I tried to retrieve the small package, it fell out onto the deck. He bent down quickly, grabbed the drugs, and tossed them over the side to the pier. That was the best way to dispose of evidence. The Master-at-Arms yelled to me to get down on the pier and get the drugs for future testimony. I knew in my mind that this was a fool's errand. I did as I was told and scrambled down the accommodation ladder to the pier.

There had to be a million Pakistanis down there conducting business as usual. I could see no package of drugs lying on the pier. So, just for kicks, I asked a couple of them standing near the ship where it probably landed if they had seen the drugs. They were professionals (drug providers), and they knew just what to say . . . nothing. All they did was look up, and one even whistled innocently.

They were so uninvolved in anything illegal, that sugar would not melt in their mouths. Whoever picked it up would be selling it back to another sailor within the hour.

In addition to helping on the quarterdeck, I had to witness a couple strip searches. These are not my cup of tea. Any time I could get out of it I did. I guess it reminded me too much of my enlistment physical, right down to the spread your cheeks part. I now know that I do not care to be on either side of that inspection. I did not even like looking at the faces on these guys. Why did I have to have them spread their cheeks for inspection? Now there was an eye I never wanted to see, even if it had been blue, which, of course, it was not.

During the time I spent onboard the USS *La Salle (AGF-3)* we visited Iran and had a change-of-command there; we crossed the equator and all aboard became shellbacks. A shellback is a person who has crossed the equator by boat or, in some instances, an old sailor. We also went through a five-month yard period in Subic Bay, Philippines. While in Subic I became friendly with a few Filipinos. When in the yards there you can get some extra things done with a carton of cigarettes. The only time in my career that I bought cigarettes was in the Subic ship repair facility. There was always that small welding job that needed to be done yesterday but was not on the work orders. Maybe something could be done to help the guys on the deckplates do their jobs better. A pack, or a carton, of cigarettes, and the Filipino welder could take his break in your space, and the job magically gets done. So, over the course of the yard period and trading smokes for favors I got to know a little about some of them. This was in 1976, and some of the workers remembered the Japanese occupation. I liked to talk with them about that time frame. I have always been interested in history, and here I was right in the middle of where a lot of it took place. The guy I knew the best was about my father's age. My dad was on a submarine in the South Pacific during part of the war, so this gentleman was old enough to know some stories.

I said to him one day, "Hey, you must've been glad to see the US return, huh?" I was referring to the expulsion of Japanese forces from the Philippines by the return of American forces, led by General Douglas MacArthur. He was slow to respond, and I thought he was looking for the words to properly express what he felt. He was.

Slowly he said, "One occupying force replacing another, and then the first force comes back. Occupation is occupation." He smiled at me and changed the subject. His comment has stayed with me through the years because I had never looked at it like that. Apparently not everyone sees us as the avenging angels coming to save the world. But no matter what you think, some things on this big blue marble are a lot better because of Americans. I am damn proud to be one.

Something that really impressed me during my stay in Subic Bay was the way the local population handled the monsoon season. I had never seen so much rain. There was a total downpour, 24/7 for about forty days. Yeah, I started looking for an ark. I saw a lot of sailors buying clear plastic raincoats and pants to stay dry. The Navy Exchange store must have made a killing. So I spent some of my hard-earned drinking money on rain gear to stay dry . . . it did not work. I was wetter with the rain gear than I was without it. It was hot and humid, and the raincoat and pants just made you sweat your balls off, so you got just as wet. The difference is that without the coat you got some air movement, whereas with the coat you stewed in your own juices.

After thirty-some days I think that the US Navy ground to a halt. There was too much water; it was coming down way too fast, and it was flooding everything. It was so wet that we all had moss growing in a lot of strange places on our bodies. I think some of the crew was starting to develop gills.

As the US Navy slowed almost to a stop, the Filipinos just kept on with their normal business as usual routine. At least that is how it looked to me.

Crossing the equator is a time-honored ritual among sailors the world over. Tradition has it that those who have not crossed and been initiated will be known as "pollywogs." While those who have mastered the bounding main will henceforth be known by all as "shellbacks." Of course, what would an honor be without the earning of that honor through some kind of initiation? *La Salle* left the yards and went on a shakedown cruise to shake out the bugs and while out crossed the equator at Latitude 00000 and Longitude 105-30E, not far from the Philippines. The pollywogs, including myself, were fairly tortured for the two-day period going across the equator. Coming back was a different story because the entire crew was already shellbacks. A few of the local Filipino yard workers were allowed to participate in the initiation too, so they became shellbacks.

Crawling the length of the ship, five hundred-plus feet, the lowly 'wogs experienced all sorts of indignities along the way.

Like most initiations, this one was made to embarrass the crap out of you. We had to crawl the length of the ship on our hands and knees, crossing over the nonskid surface and tearing our dungarees to shreds. The whole route was covered by shillelagh-wielding shellbacks bent on getting revenge for having to go through this same thing the last time *La Salle* crossed the equator. As we were herded through the ship, we were constantly slapped with the shillelaghs. When the line got to the stern, each 'wog had to go before the court of Neptunus Rex, Ruler of the Raging Main. We were found just barely qualified to be called Honorable Shellbacks. Davey Jones, His Majesty's scribe, entered our names into the log, and we were now officially shellbacks. That is it in a nutshell. There was a lot more to it than just that; however, more of the story will have to wait for volume 2 of my recollection.

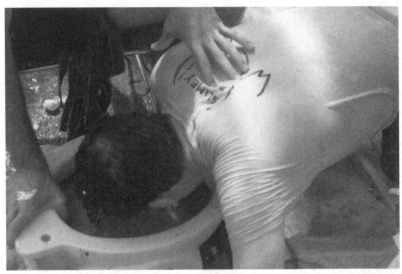

Toward the end of the crawl. I wonder how many guys before me lost their stomach in this toilet. It did not really taste all that bad.

Incidentally, the *World English Dictionary* includes this reference; "shillelagh *or* shillala (in Ireland) a stout club or cudgel, esp. one made of oak or blackthorn." In our case, they were made from three-foot-long sections of fire hose. One end was wrapped with duct tape to form a handle . . . the better to swing them, while the business end was left alone or sometimes frayed. If used properly, they could really sting and actually leave welts on a victim. Shipmates monitored each other and aimed toward the old buttocks. I do not remember anyone getting seriously hurt.

Chapter 13

"Onboard, on duty."

The first few years in the navy I was junior to most of the people in the shop. Because of that fact, I knew that if there was work to be done the odds were greatly in favor that I would be one of the lucky few who had to stay until the repairs were accomplished. I and a couple others became the first repair team that was called to get things fixed. We were all single and living onboard, so we were also easily found. I used to like saying to the troops,

"Onboard, On Duty;
Out of Sight, Out of Mind;
Off the Ship, Hard to Find."

Those who had families living close and went home on nonduty nights, referred to as brown baggers because some brought lunch from home in a brown lunch bag, never liked to stay late if they did not have to. Who could blame them? By the time they had families, most were senior enough to order others to stay late and work to repair any problems. They had already been through those junior years when they were expected to stay aboard and assist. I ended up having to stay and work on gear when I would much rather be out in town with my buddies or even just relaxing on the ship. If you were on board, you were on duty.

When a ship has an inspection cycle and cruise schedule to keep up, it makes downtime for mechanical failures almost impossible. To maintain ship readiness, almost every piece of down equipment must be repaired immediately. Who wants to tell the President of the United States that he cannot have a warship where and when he wants? It is an extreme embarrassment to the ship and the crew if it misses a commitment. Even worse is to miss one due to something that could have been avoided or because of equipment not properly maintained. Jobs have been lost and careers destroyed for less. If you are looking for a successful military career and smooth advancements, you understand how this system works. If it is broke, fix it! And, yes, as many people feel, there is also the school of thought that says if it is not broke, fix it too.

As a First Class Petty Officer onboard USS *Spruance (DD-963)* I witnessed this firsthand. I was the Leading Petty Officer (LPO) of "E" Division. The Engineering Department was on three section duty, which meant every third day I slept aboard and, with the duty section, maintained watch over the propulsion plant. This was the way all my ships were. I lived on three section duty for years. Since everyone had the same setup it went smoothly unless you had a chief that was on a different duty day than you. Many times the chief kept extra people aboard on his duty night, sometimes for no apparent reason. He was not going home, so he continued to work on after knockoff. So you would be assured of only getting one night out of three to go straight home. That was if the third section did not have a Chief who worked the same way too.

Depending on where you were in the inspection cycle, there are times when no one got to go home at a decent hour no matter how many duty sections you were in. If the ship was facing an upcoming Operational Propulsion Plant Examination (OPPE) you would just consider that your private life was gone until the exam was completed successfully. Other departments on the ship had their own corresponding inspections. My wife and I have talked about those days on *Spruance*, and we both remember all the times I left the ship late due to machinery troubles. We carpooled to work every day and on those days when I could not leave the ship at a normal time she could visit friends who lived close to the base. Otherwise, she would have had to wait in the car by the pier until I got off. She spent so much time over the years with our friends that it became a given that we would eat supper there.

It is easy to fall into a trap if you are a Chief or First Class who needs to get things done yesterday. As a supervisor I fell into that habit of keeping aboard those who I could rely upon. When you are under a lot of pressure and the chain of command wants it fixed as soon as possible and they are breathing down your neck, you find yourself seeking the most expedient way to effect the proper repairs. I found myself doing the same thing to others that I hated being done to me.

In the summer months of 1977, and between *La Salle* and *Spruance*, I did a stint at Great Lakes for the Gas Turbine (GS) Training Pipeline. The GS pipeline was pretty new at the time, and some of the curriculum was still in the rudimentary stage of development. I thought that it was good training, and the instructors did a decent job with the resources they had available to them.

While I was there I met a couple of Third Class POs who were also on their way to *Spruance*. That meant that I would be their first Leading Petty Officer (LPO) on a ship. Having our next command in common brought us together as a small group. One third class turned out to be one of the best friends I had in my career. He had a great career and, through hard work and integrity, he eventually moved up the ladder and retired as a Lieutenant. Sometimes a first LPO can have an effect on the future career and success of a new sailor. I would like to take some credit for giving him a good footing to start. However, if you knew him, you would know that he accomplished it all on his own. But, hey, I was there behind him rooting all the time.

As it happened, that very sailor was one of those who I relied upon. I had fallen into the trap that I so despised. I knew that when push came to shove, this guy would be able to troubleshoot faster than the others and make reliable repairs in the same fashion. And, he would not cut corners in the repair. He had become the go-to guy in the back of my head. He was not a complainer. He did his job, made his recommendations, and followed whatever decisions were made by the higher-ups.

But it cost him, as it did me earlier in my career. Time after time he and a few others were the ones called upon to stay late and work on the problems. Their families were being shortchanged in the opportunities to see their husband and father. The rest of the division stayed some after knockoff, but they were not kept as late as the A-Team. They then came back in time for morning muster.

Given my work history and my dislike of keeping the same people aboard for maintenance and repair, I am sometimes surprised at how easily I ended up in that situation. If a control console went down, it had to be repaired quickly. As it always seemed to happen, the control system developed major problems on the Friday prior to starting off on a cruise the following Monday. Nothing could stand in the way of leaving on Monday morning and on time. So everyone had to stay and had little time with family prior to a major cruise.

This is where the phrase "crunch time" was coined. It was balls-to-the-wall until everything was repaired. No one wanted to miss a ship's commitment, especially if the cause was in our department. That is exactly what happened the Friday before a cruise to the Mediterranean Sea. I went straight to the go-to team.

The final weekend before a major cruise is usually too short and too fast. There is a constant feeling that you are running out of time—that you are running out of quality time with the wife and kids. I have been out of the navy for years, and I still have that feeling at times. In the back of my mind I keep feeling that there are navy commitments that prevent me from making long-range personal plans. That is just how strong the feeling is. Unfortunately, any missed time with the family can never be reclaimed; it is just gone. Nobody really wanted to stay on the ship that last weekend before a major deployment. When I assembled the group who were going to do the repairs, I noticed the long faces. I knew what they were thinking; I wanted to go home too. The control consoles are mission essential and needed to be repaired. That fact did not make staying any easier to swallow. As they were getting tools and equipment ready, the third class I mentioned above, the one I became friends with, asked if he and I could talk. I said yes, and we went to another compartment where it was quiet.

"Why do the same people always have to stay?" he asked.

"Well," I said, probably wanting to get this over with and get them working, "I guess we should discuss this." We sat down and discussed the need for ship readiness to take priority over other concerns. But, he knew that, and he knew that we were all staying to get the problem resolved. He was not complaining about staying aboard; he understood that part. I decided there that he was making sense about various people sharing the overtime duties.

His question—"Why do the same people always have to stay?"—hit me like a ton of bricks. I realized that I had fallen into the same trap others had by relying on a core group of troops to make critical repairs. Once I was aware of what I was doing, I made some changes in the following years. I always tried to remember that lesson in the future, and I think I did a fair job of it. In the future I shared the wealth of repairs with everyone to the best of my ability. Remember that I said I did it to "the best of my ability." It was not always possible or prudent to work that way. Now I knew how other supervisors had fallen so easily into the same trap. So, all things taken into consideration, I had learned the lesson from both the worker and the supervisor views.

Throughout my navy career I worked for, with, and over some really great technicians. I have always been proud of my ability to get along with just about anyone. That skill helped on numerous occasions when interacting with two men from polar opposite backgrounds and temperaments. One of the most difficult jobs I had was being the conduit between two officers who disliked each other. Both were great officers, good family men, and exceptional at their jobs, and for some reason unknown to me they could not stand each other. These two Department Heads would periodically have to deal directly with each other. In one case I acted as the go-between. It was a few rough hours, but it paid off to not have them in the same room at the same time. Everything was ironed out, and life continued. I never asked or found out what the beef between them was. They did not answer to me.

Chapter 14

"You've got the handcuffs on upside down!"

Shore Patrol entered my life again during a visit to Toulon, France. This time the SP band was on my shoulder. The band is made of black material with the letters S and P on it so anyone can see that you have pulled shore patrol for that night. Most ships have designated personnel that usually fulfill the need when it arises. I did not get SP duty very often because I worked in the engineering spaces, and usually in port there were repairs or preventative maintenance to be performed. I do not know that that is written down anywhere, but that seems to be how it worked for me during my career.

Before I get to Toulon, however, there are a couple of side notes.

I may have been the first Gas Turbine Systems Technician to pull SP duty in Rota, Spain. Or course, that and two dollars and fifty cents might get you a cup of coffee. Just like seeking any port in a storm, sometimes you have to search for a claim to fame. Hey, this is my only claim, so I take it.

Let me explain. In October 1977 the navy officially folded designated personnel from other rates or job descriptions into the Gas Turbine rating. The designation was given to anyone who had graduated from the Gas Turbine Pipeline prior to that date. Prior to that, the job was being done by a number of other ratings. These included ratings such as Enginemen, Electrician, and Machinist Mate, along with a couple others. I was an Electrician's Mate First

94

Class, and I knew since the day I graduated from the GS pipeline in Great Lakes that eventually the navy would take that action.

There was no surprise to the initial six hundred men navywide that it was going to happen. That is what we had all been working toward. That is why the navy spent all that money putting us through the training. As of October 1, 1977, we had to change our rating badge from what we were to the new GS badge, and I became Gas Turbine Systems Technician—Electrical First Class (GSE1).

When the change came we were already crossing the Atlantic headed toward Rota. I am sure we all had uniforms ready to go. The USS *Spruance* was the first Gas Turbine Destroyer to enter Rota, Spain. I guess I got SP duty that night because I had recently checked aboard and was the least knowledgeable about the engineering plant. I ended up being assigned to the Enlisted Men's (EM) Club.

The EM Club is not to be confused with the Electrician's Mate rating. I made that mistake during my newbie days on my very first visit to the EM Club at Quonset Point Naval Air Station. Since I graduated from Electrician's Mate Class "A" (EM "A") School, I constantly heard the phrase EM . . . that, and EM . . . this, and so on. Every instance was concerning my rating. One day a bunch of us went to the Enlisted Men's Club for lunch. I looked around and was struck by the number of people having lunch. I said to the Petty Officer sitting next to me, "Man, there's a lot of electricians here."

He did not really say anything to me except maybe, "Yeah, whatever, Bootcamp."

We ate our lunch, and I listened while they talked about women, booze, and women and booze. After everyone paid their tabs, and we were walking out the door heading back to the *Wasp*, I said to no one in particular, "That's a nice club for just electricians." It was as if the world had stopped turning.

My group included about five or six guys plus me. They all stopped in unison, turned, and looked at me with these big shit-eating grins. "Hey, Boot, what did you just say?" Then they were falling all over themselves from laughing. "EM stands for Enlisted Men's Club, stupid." The laughing continued. "Did you think everybody in the club were electricians? Oh, man, can you guys believe that?"

"Well," I said, "the sign just says EM Club." That was embarrassing enough, but I was about to learn what "being in the barrel" meant. I was the butt of all jokes for quite a while in the shop where I worked. I was looking down the barrel of a gun, and every so often someone took a shot at me with a joke or two. The jokes usually ended with me being stupid somehow. I could not wait until some other guy in the shop screwed up and took my place in the barrel. I took up prayer after that—"Oh, God, please let someone else screw up soon, *please!*"

The night I was assigned to the Rota Enlisted Men's Club was the only night the *Spruance* would be there. We had an early morning underway time scheduled. As I walked around the club keeping an eye on things I garnered the attention of a number of customers. A fellow First Class stopped me and asked, "What are you, a Wagon Wheel One?" He was referring to the rating badge on my sleeve. The GS rating badge is supposed to be a turbine that is sucking and blowing. That is what a turbine does. It sucks air in, and it blows air out. Since we were the first GS ship in Rota after the changeover and since I was the first off the ship, I feel strongly that I was the first to hit the ground as a GS in Rota, Spain. Cool, huh? Now, what rewards have I reaped from that distinction? Not a freakin' thing! Nice story, but who gives a crap?

My night as shore patrol in Toulon was nothing to laugh at. Other than being in the duty section I have no idea how I was picked for that night. The First Class Master-at-Arms was a friend of mine, and he had limited resources as far as equipment went. The four or five of us from *Spruance* were each given armbands and nightsticks. The one set of handcuffs he had he gave to me. We were driven by the SP carryall van to the SP office they had in town. A Marine Sergeant Major was the one in charge that night. When he inventoried equipment and found out that I was the only one with handcuffs he said right away, "You're with me." How lucky for me that would turn out.

Toulon, France, is a big city, and it is great liberty. I have been there a couple of times and have enjoyed each visit. Part of the allure is the French women for the single guys. I always liked to sightsee the local area. When nighttime came we were all out in town eating, drinking, and drinking some more. I could not indulge while on SP duties, but the rest of the fleet, which included an Amphibious Landing Aircraft Carrier, was in full party mode. That is spelled "P-A-R-T-Y-!!!" The sergeant major and I walked our rounds like all the others. When it started to get pretty late, the drunks became a lot to handle. I am not saying this was an old marine, but he had been around quite a while. No matter what his age was, I pity the idiot that tried to get something over on him. He looked as though he was all muscle. Well, the idiot showed up.

There was a minor riot in a club on a side street. We got the call to go and assist. The Sergeant Major was ready to kick some ass. He said that he was too old to fool around with these guys. When ten or twelve SPs showed up, a lot of the mob kind of disappeared into the night. The idiot I mentioned, however, stood his ground. I do not know what his rank was, but he was a sailor. He was a stupid sailor. He stood in the middle of the small courtyard and was flailing his arms like the Tasmanian Devil. Four of us grappled with him to get control and stop his arms. The marine pulled me out and said, "Get the cuffs ready."

Before I knew it, they had him in a hold that left his hands behind his back. His mouth still worked, and he started spitting at and on everybody he could reach. They got him turned around, and the Sergeant Major said, "Get 'em on quick!" By now he was spitting and kicking wildly at everyone. I tried to avoid the kicks but still got hit a few times, and my shoes took a beating. When the cuffs were on him, and he was in a headlock hold, we dragged him down the street to the office, where some big SPs were waiting for him.

When we got there he started kicking and spitting again while I tried to unlock the handcuffs. I could not figure out why I could not get the key into the little hole. I know you are all thinking about "little hole" jokes. But this was not funny. Finally the marine came back to help. Man, was he ticked off at me.

He said, "You've got the handcuffs on upside down!" I could tell right away that he would love to have me in his unit for disciplinary measures. I remembered what my basic-training Company Commander had said one day: "You're STUPID!"

To remove the restraints meant that I had to get below his hands and try to get the key up into the cuffs. After a few tries and a lot more kicking, I finally got them unlocked. I took a beating that night, and I wondered if the marine had let him kick me more than necessary. I never saw either of them again, so it does not matter. The opinion that the Sergeant Major had of sailors took a nosedive that day. I walked away hoping that I would never get shore patrol duty again.

I had another brief encounter with the marines on another occasion. We were on liberty looking for a cold beer. As we walked down the street in this port, we passed a group of marines going in the opposite direction. As we passed, one of them said to me, "Excuse me, First Class," referring to my uniform and rank. "There's a decent bar ahead of you on the right. You might want to stop there; the beer is cold."

"Thank you, Corporal, I appreciate it," I said back to him, and we continued in our respective directions.

Later that night I happened into a bar, and there was a fight going on. It was more verbal than physical. I still try to stay away from drunken brawls, and my group started to leave. As we did, one of the marines stopped his part in the calamity and said to me, "Sorry, First Class. We'll take it outside." It was not the same marine who told us about the cold beer. If you knew me you would know that I am not a particularly tough guy. In fact, I have never won an honest fight in my life. I was pretty impressed with myself, however, because I could not believe the training these marines must go through. Just seeing my first-class rating badge made him straighten up. Too bad I never met a sailor like that.

I used to joke with my buddies about never winning a fair fight in my life. So if I ever get mad at you, I will wait until you are dead drunk in your rack and facedown. Then I will get the biggest knife I can find and stab you in the back multiple times. Do not screw with me.

Chapter 15

"The navy only made you an E-7 . . ."

Serving in one branch of the military is pretty much like serving in the other branches. There are, of course, the obvious differences between the US Army and the US Navy. Very simply put, the navy patrols the seas, and the army patrols the land masses. An army acquaintance of mine used to take great pleasure in his claim that the army had more ships than the navy. That may be the case given the transports, cargo vessels, hospital ships, and watercraft they have at their disposal. I suspect that not many of their ships can land a jet fighter. The differences between the navy and all the other branches are many. The enlisted ranking structure has always confounded me. Each service uses the same pay scale, which goes from E-1 through E-9. To the best of my knowledge only the navy treats the step from E-6 to E-7 as a major departure from the status quo.

Going from First Class Petty Officer (E-6) to Chief Petty Officer (E-7) takes a sailor into another whole world. This is where the crew member moves out of the junior enlisted quarters and into the Chiefs' Mess. The uniform changes from working uniform, dungarees in my days, to khakis. Most people take on a whole new persona and garner renewed respect from their peers. Now they must be prepared when someone says, "Go ask the Chief." Personnel junior and senior to them now come to them for assistance and advice. Once you are in the Chief Petty Officers' (CPO) Mess you find that many interdivisional and departmental problems are solved there over a cup of good old navy coffee.

I have never been a proponent of navy coffee, however, because I like cream and sugar in my coffee and do not like it as strong as most messes make. I am a real man and not afraid to admit that I want cream and sugar in my coffee . . . so there. Some guys would sit and drink that horrible coffee just so they would not be ribbed about it being "pussy coffee." A real man is not hesitant to fix it the way he likes it. Take note, it is my opinion that if you put your spoon in the coffee, and it stands straight up without touching the side of the cup, that's too damn strong!

The truth is that I was in the navy for ten years before I took a liking to coffee. A lot of people pick up the habits of cigarettes and coffee within the first few months of joining. I suffered through ten years' worth of mid-watches before I broke down and started drinking java through necessity. I never have smoked.

Since so many things change for navy personnel when they make the upward move from Petty Officer to Chief Petty Officer, it can be equated with joining a new club. Like many clubs or organizations, there is an initiation to be passed before you are accepted by the rank and file. There is a real difference between being appointed an E-7 by the US Navy and being considered a Chief by other members of the Mess. That is where the initiation becomes the doorway to being a Chief in the Chiefs' Mess. Chief Petty Officers treat other CPOs with a certain respect that would be withheld from a mere E-7. Throughout my years in the navy I have seen countless times when a Chief will tell a newly promoted E-7 that, "The Navy only made you an E-7. The Chiefs' Mess will make you a Chief!"

When news of the promotion to E-7 comes through, it usually is ahead of the date on which it becomes official. That makes the candidate a "Selectee" or "Chief Selectee" until the official date is reached. There will be weeks before you put on the uniform of a CPO and try to act like one. During that time frame, the above-mentioned initiation is being carried out. Not many clubs have an initiation that takes weeks. It is precisely during that period when the Selectee will have his mettle tested. Some have likened it to being a first-year Plebe at the academy only not so easy.

When I participated in my own initiation in 1981, it was conducted differently than today's navy handles them. So, when I speak of these things I speak from my own experience. I wonder how many times that last sentence will be used in this book before I am done?

I have it on good authority that much of what was accepted as part of the fun when I was initiated is deemed too politically incorrect in today's navy. In the past sometimes these affairs got out of control and injuries were incurred by some of the selectees. These injuries usually happened the last day, at the actual initiation ceremony. The weeks leading up to that point were, to me, where the damage really occurred. From mid-July to mid-September it seemed as though my initiation was twenty-four hours and seven days a week.

During the weeks that the selectees are waiting for their collar devices to be pinned on, there are certain things they must suffer through. These include various tasks and indignities placed upon them by CPOs to test their abilities to take orders, maintain a cool head, and be humble when necessary to accomplish the mission. Unfortunately, another thing we were required to do was to have with us at all times a CPO Charge Book. The Charge Book usually consisted of an official green general purpose logbook with a heavy chain attached to it. Each command provided any directions on decorating these books per the desires of the Chiefs' Mess. The chain was used to secure the book to our persons.

So we Selectees walked around with this heavy chain and book, which we presented to any Chief who asked for it. They, in turn, would write into the book any real or imagined slight we had made against humanity. Later, the book was examined and charges made out against us based on what had been entered. On the final day of initiation the Chiefs held court (can you say kangaroo); we had to work off the charges made. That is the part most selectees fear the most.

I, however, held a different take on the whole thing. By the time it was all over and we were finally accepted as Chief Petty Officers, I was so incredibly tired of being harassed by Chiefs. I seriously wondered if I really wanted to be one. I thought they were all a bunch of assholes without a lick of maturity. This might be a club I did not want to join. I am not going into details of exactly what happened to me or other selectees because that type of information belongs in the Chiefs' Mess. What happens in the Chiefs' Mess stays in the Chiefs' Mess. Suffice it to say that they hound you over and over and irritate the crap out of you. Nothing gets them off more than you losing your composure. I was very good at maintaining my cool, but I did lose it a couple of times.

When I made Chief in 1981, I was stationed at the Twenty-Hotel-Five (20H5) training simulator in Norfolk, Virginia. The DD-963 Engineering Console Simulator was located in the Electrician's Mate Class "C" School building. That building also housed the Pre-Commissioning Units (PRECOM) of a number of ships. 20H5 was at the end of a building wing. It was the same wing that just happened to share a common parking lot with the base liquor store. That was one convenience I enjoyed in the navy that I always appreciated. Enough said along that line.

As one of the Leading Petty Officers at 20H5, my duties required that I visit the "C" School's Administration Office as well as the School Director's Office several times a day. That was not a particular hardship, but, it did mean I had to transit through the Pre-Comm area. There, lying in wait to ambush me each and every time, were Chiefs who had nothing to do except hassle me. These were CPOs who had a command but no physical ship yet and were basically reduced to taking muster and ensuring field day was held daily. All their pent-up "Chief" energy that would normally be directed toward shipboard duties was now aimed at me. So, every day I walked the gauntlet trying to perform my duties. As I went down the long hall from Chief to Chief being berated for imagined crimes and misdemeanors against the world of CPOs I got madder and madder each time. It was a constant hell, and there was no relief in sight for me.

One day I found myself being viciously, in my mind anyway, dressed down. This Chief was really feeling his oats. He yelled and screamed up one side and down the other. I think he even spit on me by accident. His face had the appearance of an angry Doberman. His breath smelled like one too. Before I knew what was happening, my jaws got very tight, and I started rocking back and forth on the balls of my feet. My face must have been extremely red. Of course, this did not go unnoticed by the Chief. This only incensed him more. He knew he had me, and it was probably like Christmas for him. He got as close as humanly possible and raised the pitch of his voice.

He screamed at me, "Do I piss you off, shithead?" He continued with "Do you wanna hit me?"

"YES!" I yelled back at him. "YES!"

He got this big smile on his face and calmly retorted, "Well, go for it, Chief."

That is when I realized what was going on and started to mentally and physically spin down. He had gotten what he wanted and was done. I felt and probably looked like an idiot. Well, maybe he had a cup of coffee and a donut waiting somewhere, so he left me standing in the hallway. As he walked off he said over his shoulder, "Get the fuck outta here."

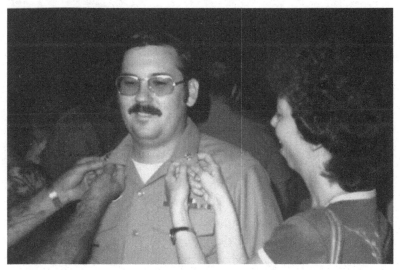

September 1981. Master Chief of 20H5 and my wife Donna pinning on my first collar devices. I looked pretty good for a guy who had not eaten identifiable food in almost twenty-four hours.

What was remarkable to me was that the same energy they used, in the weeks leading up to the actual initiation ceremony to harass me, they used to welcome me into the chiefs community. Once it was all over and we were wearing our collar devices, it was as though we were old friends with the rest of the chiefs in the world. All was right in the world of the US Navy CPOs, and secretly the former selectees, those newly made chiefs, could not wait for the next year's group of selectees. Yeah, me too! Paybacks anyone?

Say hello to the new Chief. Gas Turbine System Technician—
Electrical (GSEC) Bishop and his lovely wife, Donna.

The initiation is not required by the navy and can be refused. If an E-7 chooses not to participate, he or she may not be warmly welcomed in the Chiefs' Mess. They will always be treated in a professional manner and duties will be performed as required at all times. Mission readiness will not suffer because of a refusal to go through the initiation process.

I can only remember one E-7 who refused to participate in the initiation. He was stationed on a ship that came through Guantanamo Bay, Cuba, for training while I was an instructor there. The Chiefs were not overly unkind to him, but they were not overly kind to him either. He was treated almost like a pariah of sorts. Nothing interfered with training. The entire CPO Mess acted professionally toward him and the job at hand. I am sure that it must have been very uncomfortable for him. For my money, it could not have been worth it.

In the hierarchy of the US military, rank has its privileges, or RHIP, as we used to say. The way it manifests itself is not always obvious. Take the chow line onboard any sea command. During each meal the engineering spaces cycle their personnel through the chow line and try to ensure everyone gets fed. Given the workload standard in those spaces, it is seldom that everyone gets through the line. When they do get up to eat there are menu cards that spell out how much each person gets. So when a sailor goes through the line his meal is doled out in accordance with the menu card. Here is a twenty-something, muscular, still-growing man who has his peas counted out, his fish patty the exact size, and a scoop of pudding dropped on his tray and sent on his way. He wolfs down his food and goes back to work, seconds seldom allowed.

On the other side of the galley is a door leading to the Chiefs' Mess. This is a totally different situation. In the good old days, my days, the Chief was served by a Messcook and could have seconds or even thirds. In addition, there is always something to pick on in the CPO Mess such as donuts, cookies, and other things. Police officers have nothing on Navy Chiefs when it comes to coffee and donuts.

So here is the Chief, who is probably in his thirties, already getting a gut, remember I speak from experience, and not as active as he once was, eating anything he wants and whenever he would like. If he gets hungry later he simply goes back to the mess for a quick bite. Is there any wonder that Chiefs start to look like the stereotypical CPO as seen in comics and jokes? I only say this because I can no longer enjoy that benefit. I do miss that part.

It was while stationed at the 20H5 Trainer that I got one of the best compliments I believe I ever received on active duty. The office I worked in had five or six instructors assigned to it at any given time. There were also about three technicians who worked on the trainer itself. Since it was a relatively new facility, there were not a lot of students coming through, and we were still developing curriculum. As we worked there each day a lot of the conversations turned to the technical aspects of our rating and sea stories about what had happened on our respective ships. Sea stories aside, we had some spirited discussions about the way to perform our duties when at sea.

Apparently I did not contribute to the debates as much as I could or should have. I guess that I always felt that most of the other participants were more qualified than I was to speak on the subject. The others were always so sure of their convictions that I had no real desire to dispute any of the finer points and get roped into a never-ending battle of who was right and who was wrong. So, I just listened to a lot of the discussions, and my silence was noticed.

One thing I did contribute to the workday was a sense of humor. Since the day I drew my first breath I have always tried to find the comedy in every situation. If there is one thing that I am most proud of, it is my sense of humor. I wonder how many people reading this are thinking to themselves, "*That guy* has a sense of humor?" No one can ever take that away from me. Now, I have had some moments during stressful periods when I did not find much to laugh at, but for the most part I kept them laughing.

The 20H5 Trainer was no exception. I could always find a joke or other reason to laugh. So we spent a lot of time laughing while we worked. Everybody assigned to that office had a good sense of the absurd, and laughter is contagious. One day the Master Chief said to me, "Bishop, you're about an average technician, but, Goddamn it, if you ain't the best thing for morale I ever saw!"

I take that as a great compliment. Another even greater one came to me recently from an unsolicited source. A former shipmate told me in an e-mail that he remembers how rough things were on one of our ships. He said the troops were pretty down. He also said that I brought the humor back to the department when I checked aboard. As much as an exaggeration as that might be, you cannot believe how nice it was to hear that from a guy I have not seen in years. He was not the only guy who has said something along that line to me since I retired, and they have all made me feel good. I will be happy if I am only remembered for my ability to find humor in the strangest places.

Chapter 16

"Ya know how to make a shark disappear?"

I consider all my duty stations unique and memorable. But, if I had to point out one of the more memorable, and certainly most unique, tours of duty, I would have to say Guantanamo Bay, Cuba, was it. As I mentioned prior to this, I was stationed there as an instructor. Quite a few sailors visit GTMO each year, but very few actually are stationed there and live on base. It was a once-in-a-lifetime opportunity. I was transferred to Cuba in 1983 and had been a Chief for two years.

One of the things that struck me immediately about life in Cuba was the laid-back atmosphere. We lived in base housing so, other than keeping the house clean and the lawn cut, there was not much to do to the house inside or outside. Some minor projects could be completed to make the tour a little more comfortable. An example is the home entertainment unit a fellow chief helped me build. Actually, I helped him build it. He had all the woodworking tools and the know-how to do that big a project. I did some other things around the house, but, again, there was not much to do.

Chief Bishop and wife Donna in front of Chiefs' Club in Guantanamo Bay Naval Station, Cuba. We enjoyed the laid-back lifestyle while stationed there.

On the base were a number of clubs and organizations. I joined The Reef Raiders and learned to scuba dive. That was one of the best decisions I have ever made. I learned to dive in what has to be one of the most pristine and beautiful areas of the underwater world. Visibility was phenomenal, even at one hundred feet, where the surface seemed to be only a few feet above you. My dive partner and I went as many times as we could. We just flat enjoyed it. Unfortunately, after I returned to the states I could not bring myself to try and continue diving. I was always afraid that the experience in the local area and the poor visibility would ruin it for me. As a result, the only place I talk about having gone diving is in GTMO.

Diving in Guantanamo Bay was great. But there were some problems associated with it. Part of the training was night diving. When you dive at night the visibility is not as good as daylight, but sometimes the moon is full, and the cloudless sky gives the dive a serene atmosphere. It is almost as if God had switched on a light somewhere. You could turn off your dive light and enjoy the eerie illumination. Sometimes the light had to stay on because the moon was not so bright.

Before one of my earlier night dives, during the pre-dive meeting, we were discussing the rowdy denizens of the deep, barracudas and sharks. These two aquatic bullies were very prevalent in the waters around the US Naval Station, GTMO, and everyone wanting to dive Cuba needed to be aware of this. Every day a diver would run into a shark or something else just as unnerving. I have heard it said that firing a speargun in the ocean around the base was like ringing a dinner bell for the sharks. If a diver is spearfishing and is approached by a shark, he will generally give the fish he has caught to the shark and move away. With so many divers in the water the sharks have gotten used to seeing humans around and about every reef. So, like Pavlov's dog, the shark is responding to the sound of fish being speared, and he knows the diver will gladly give the catch to him. Or, so the story goes. The part about the diver with the spear and the shark is scuttlebutt I have heard.

One of my fellow divers one night was the Master Chief who I worked for. He was another supervisor who had a positive influence on me throughout the course of my career. I have deep respect for him as well as the other instructors I worked with. As we prepared for the dive and got to the point of checking the gear on each other's back, the conversation returned to deadly fish. Custom is that every diver checks his dive buddy's equipment prior to the dive. Making sure regulators, hoses, fins, vest, and the like have no apparent problems. When my partner got to my dive knife and light he chuckled. I looked at him to see what was so funny.

He said, "What are you gonna to do with the knife? Gonna fend off sharks if they get too close tonight?"

I waved my empty left hand in the sign of a "Z" a la Zorro. "You bet I am." Then, after smiling back at him, I said "No, of course I'm not." Fact is, I never used a dive knife for anything other than banging it on my tank to get someone's attention. I believe that is pretty standard throughout the diving community. The weapon does have a purpose, however. It is used to cut something that you get caught on, to dig in the sea floor when you are looking for something, and to bang on your tank. Self-defense against ocean critters is not a sanctioned use. But who knows in an emergency what you might have to try.

Now that the knife discussion was taken care of and the other equipment was ready, we started toward the dark water to make the night dive. As we got to the water's edge he looked at me and said seriously, "Ya know how to make a shark disappear?" I waited for the answer. "Turn off your light."

While diving one day with just one dive buddy I started to feel anxious about something that I could not explain. I still do not know what was happening to me. We were diving from one of the secluded beaches and were alone. We had gone to the depth of one hundred feet and were picking up conch shells. Suddenly I started to feel panicked and was getting pretty nervous. My fellow diver was next to me but could not tell that anything was wrong. Suddenly I remembered what the dive instructor had said to do in a situation like this.

"Pull yourself into a fetal position. That seems to clear it up."

That is exactly what I did, and he was right; my mind did start to clear, and a minute later all was normal. My dive buddy was not aware of what just happened. I look back on it and realize that he could only be a good dive buddy if I kept him in the loop, so to speak. That incident also reminded me of what the instructor at Fire Fighting School had said about putting my nose to the hose. It was sage advice from two great instructors. You never know when a past lesson will come in handy.

Another unique thing about this area of Cuba is the Guantanamo River that flows through the bay we used for our operations. It was strange to see a Soviet ship passing right through the middle of the US naval base. In order to get goods from the ocean to Guantanamo City, ships had to utilize the river to transit up through the gate and on to the city. There was a water gate that stopped unauthorized vessels from going onto Cuba proper. When arrangements were made to slip through the US base, they notified US authorities and the Cuban personnel in charge of the gate. Any activity by the US Navy was temporarily halted until the foreign ship had passed.

On days when training was not being conducted, sailors from the ships visiting GTMO for that purpose were free to utilize whatever base facilities they cared to. Some spent time at one of the fleet beaches, the ships threw parties for their crews, or some would rent a boat from Welfare and Recreation. Boats could be used for fishing, diving, just enjoying the bay, or a number of other recreational purposes.

Every so often one of those boats would stray too close or actually go into Cuban-controlled waters. I am sure the boat ride took on a different feel when the Cuban military arrested the American sailors. The route they took back from the water gate to their ship was a lot longer than the ride they had from the ship to GTMO City in the first place. As far as I know they were returned via diplomatic procedures. They probably got back to the ship by way of Havana, the embassy of a neutral country, Washington, the US Navy, and their Commanding Officer. Every step in the process was a bunch of chuckles, I am sure.

In Guantanamo Bay we lived in crowded isolation. We were on a naval base with a number of separate commands, at least one air wing and all the support personnel and equipment that it required to run an operation that large. Even so, we were isolated because we could not leave the base. Surrounding the base was a mini-Iron Curtain. It was used as a means of protection against we Americans scaling the fence and taking Guantanamo City by force.

When you think of Cuba you probably think of lush forests and jungles. The area of Cuba where the American base is located is in the driest and most desert-like portion of the whole island nation. To my thinking, there is nothing on the other side of the fence that I would want to take by force. If the gate was opened I am sure the sailors would find entertainment somewhere in town. I personally think that that will eventually happen and our two countries will again pursue diplomatic relations in the future. I have no concrete evidence that friendlier relations between the United States and Cuba will someday return. I simply feel that as the Cuban leadership ages the time for changes will come about. I hope so.

When Fidel Castro took power in the 1960s, relations between the naval facility and Cuba proper were suspended indefinitely. The gates leading out into the local area were all closed. I would be surprised if the local economy did not suffer a lot without US sailors spending their money in the bars and shops there. A few Cuban nationals living in town had jobs on the naval station, and through some agreement were allowed by both governments to come and go through the gate each workday. I understand that they are searched each way for contraband. There are not that many of these transients left because as they die off they cannot be replaced, as part of the agreement.

Those of us who have lived in Guantanamo Bay know that any discussion of the life down there would not be complete without at least a mention of the voracious insect known as "*teeth*!" Be afraid; be very afraid. There are T-shirts that say, "I survived *teeth* in GTMO." The shirts include an artist's conception of what they look like. To truly envision one, just picture in your mind a giant set of teeth flying around. That is it, no body, just teeth, and teeth with wings. In reality these things are so small you can barely see them. Normal screens do not stop them from getting into your house. I am surprised that closed windows keep them out. Every day around dusk they come out to feed. Suddenly, you feel something bite the loving crap right out of you. You have to experience them to believe them.

Every couple of weeks a barge would be towed into the naval base with supplies from the States. The next few days were almost like Christmas for the residents. That is when the fresh produce got to the shelves of the commissary, and it would be a first-come, first-served situation. The Navy Exchange also got its new items, and it was another first-come operation too. Everything coming to GTMO and too large to mail came by barge—autos, furniture, and other household goods, and, by the time I left, supplies for the new McDonald's being built. The burger chain opened just before my departure, but I never got inside it.

Another phenomenon that was part of life in GTMO was the proliferation of video movie exchanges between residents. Almost every household had a library of movies that they used to share with other households. Every format you could find was represented on the base. Lists were circulated around the naval station of which movies each person had so you could contact them and trade or borrow films to watch. I started to build a movie library while stationed there and today have quite an extensive one, much to my lovely wife's chagrin.

Fellow Officers and Chiefs at Fleet Training Group, GTMO.
An outstanding bunch of guys.

The biggest memory for me from GTMO was a health issue that reared its ugly head while I was there. Somehow, I contracted a tropical disease while in Cuba. I know, it sounds like the start of a dirty joke. It manifested itself with massive cysts all over the body, and in my case in the groin area. At the time I was placed in an isolation unit at Portsmouth Naval Hospital, Portsmouth, Virginia. I had about seventeen cysts in that area at one time. These were very painful. After a week and a half I got out of the hospital but had to stay stateside for an additional month because Cuba was too hot for me to recover properly there.

The good news was that I got a month of convalescence leave in the States. The bad news was that kind of time can get pretty expensive. When I finally got back to the naval station in Cuba I was still supposed to stay out of the hot spaces on the ships. That was what my job was. I was assigned to Fleet Training Group (FTG) training ships in engineering casualty control procedures. Watchstanders were trained with refresher exercises of mechanical problems they were likely to face at sea. They had to know what actions to take to save the equipment, the ship, and the personnel on board.

This important training helped crews respond in the event a major piece of machinery broke down or there was a fire or other casualty in an engineering space. It provided me with a great opportunity to meet some really sharp sailors. These were people who a guy could learn a lot from. I learned something from every ship we trained. I worked with some sharp sailors, too, but do not tell them I said that.

One of my big regrets from my time in the navy was that I could have taken the opportunity I was presented with here to train and qualify to hold drills in the Central Control Station (CCS) but I did not. That would have been a step up for me. But things were not good health-wise for me during my tour down there. I did not realize what the problems were, but I was already feeling the mental and physical effects of the Parkinson's disease that would get me full-on later in life. My psoriasis went crazy down there in the heat of Cuba too. There were days when I was pretty miserable. Between the diseases and the medicines, some days I could barely stay awake.

Fleet Training Group professionals during some much-needed, but rare, downtime. They look harmless out of uniform.

With all the health issues I had while there, I still look back on Guantanamo with great memories. I worked with a great group of guys across the board. The instructors at Fleet Training Group were all professionals and served the US Navy well, officers and enlisted alike.

Chapter 17

"I have the technology; I've just chosen not to use it!"

One thing that always amazed me were the various leadership styles that you find at any command. I saw everything from a leader being walked on by his men to one who could not lead at all without being a total asshole. I would like to think my own style was somewhere in the middle. I guess those I supervised would have to answer that. I remember that early in my career I was described in an evaluation as being "somewhat less than forceful." I truly liked the officer who wrote that, and I would consider him a friend even today.

He was not being malicious or intent on hurting my upward progress. As I look at it years later I am sure he was trying to give me a message. Like many in positions of authority, he felt that a good leader had to have a hard edge to his dealings with subordinates. While I can appreciate it now, at the time he could have kissed my ass as far as I was concerned. The warrant officer who wrote that was a real decent guy, and I wish only the best for him, his wife, and son.

I have always been more soft-spoken than a lot of my peers. I saw no need to become a raving lunatic just to get things done. A number of times in the Chiefs' Mess a fellow Chief would tell me that I was too easy on the troops. But the work always got done, and the ship remained mission ready.

That may be due to the efforts of the Second Class Petty Officers in the Engineering Department. In my opinion the Second Class is the backbone of the navy. Most of them are hard workers and are at ease with personnel up and down the chain of command. I always remember my days as a PO2 with satisfaction and pride. I enjoyed passing the shit bucket up or down the chain of command.

Engineering PO2s at rest. These guys were truly the backbone of the Navy. They helped keep my chestnuts out of the fire many times. There are other Second Classes not pictured here that were just as great. They know who they are.

I am sure that there were times when I got walked on by the troops. I know that there were a couple of times when I was a complete, raging asshole. In that second case the troops deserved it or I would not have done it . . . so there. I know that you have to have a relationship with the guys that keeps you somewhat distant yet affords them the chance to talk and give honest opinions. I said honest opinions; man, I hated yes-men.

When the top dog, big banana orders you to take that hill, like marines, you have to do it without question. But the first thing a sailor does is to ask if he can try to find another way. When you gotta take the hill, there is no time for questions. I never minded answering questions, but I never had an actual *take the hill* situation.

Conversations with my guys went something like this.

I said, "Would you two go to the engineroom and . . . ?" here you can fill in the blank.

They stand there for a few seconds and finally say something like, "Would we?"

Or the original request was along this line.

"How about you two guys do . . . yada, yada, yada, (Thank you, Jerry Seinfeld)."

I generally knew what was coming, and they would follow my direction to them with, "How about?" I think they enjoyed the repartee, and I would follow up with an amendment to the first order.

"All right, you two go do this . . . and let me know how it goes." I never felt that you had to be an idiot to get things done. I have nothing but respect for the sailors who worked for me. I had to because they kept my chestnuts out of the fire quite a few times. Just as they can help you, no group can put the screws to you any better than those who work for you and know where the skeletons are.

Once in a while a situation comes up that tests your ability to deal with the various personalities found in the service. The US Navy has an extremely diverse population from countless ethnic and cultural backgrounds, making for a true melting pot. Something breaks down, and it is all hands on deck until repairs are made. On those days when the troops were hard to motivate, I would let them know that we were stuck here until the problems were solved. Sometimes they might balk at another crisis to be dealt with. I generally tried to keep my humorous vein in sight, because a laugh can always help.

"Look, I'm not trying to be an asshole about this. This has to get repaired as soon as possible. I know how to be an asshole," I said. "I have the technology; I've just chosen not to use it!"

That usually got a smile or two and maybe even a laugh out loud. With a little prodding everybody got to work.

When it comes to being a team member, I felt that protection went up and down the chain. I tried to watch out for the people who worked for me, and I tried to keep egg off the face of the officers I worked for too. The theory is that I watch their backs, and they return the favor. It usually worked out that way. Like most families or teams, the Engineering Department can have all the infighting it needs, but when the threat is from the outside, the people all pulled together as a unit.

Getting up for the early watch. I look thrilled, huh? I was about to assume the watch and become part of the first line of defense for this nation. If that does not give you pause, God bless you.

The Main Propulsion Assistant (MPA) on *Yorktown* sure watched my back a few times. For some reason when I had the mid-watch in Central Control Station (CCS), I would develop an urge to make a head call. That is a potty break, for those who do not know the lingo we use on ships. Standing the mid-watch means from midnight until four in the morning. I did not need him every watch, but a number of times he came down when I called his stateroom in the middle of the night so I could make a head call. None of us were getting much sleep, and he was probably getting less than most of us. Still, every time I called, he came down to relieve me. God bless his pea-pickin' heart, he was another shipmate I was glad I served with.

He eventually went on to become an Admiral in the Pacific Fleet, I believe. I would love to have seen him in that position, because he had a great sense of humor. Imagine, an Admiral with a sense of humor. What a strange concept.

Chapter 18

"No, ma'am, they didn't. We can eat anything on the table."

One of the things I liked about being stationed on the Battlecruiser USS *Yorktown (CG-48)* was that the Captain was always showing the ship. When we pulled in at various countries he allowed the local population to go on guided tours of the non-sensitive areas. He also showed the ship to local residents of any American port we visited, which I enjoyed the most. Once when we were in Rota, Spain, I believe, the American community took tours, including the Department of Defense (DOD) School. It was pleasant to see American youth interested in our navy.

The Battlecruiser USS *Yorktown (CG-48)* underway from
Norfolk Naval Base.

The evening before the American community tour, the Wardroom and the Chiefs' Mess members went to dinner together. We did this periodically, and at that evening's dinner I happened to be sitting next to the Captain. I learned a long time ago never to let your guard down when talking to the CO of any command. Since this was my CO, I was being particularly cautious. It was a nice evening; the dinner was good, and the company was great. I held my own in the conversations across the table and managed to not say anything I would regret. At least, I thought I had stayed safe.

Somewhere during the evenings talk I made a comment to the CO that I appreciated his efforts to show the Battlecruiser to the American people. In fact, I really did appreciate it. I always thought the public should be able to see what they were paying for as far as the military was concerned. I did not know how my remark would affect me or how soon. After dinner it was getting late, and the group split up and went a dozen different directions. I stayed with one of the gangs that hit the bars. The booze was flowing freely, and we made a big night of it.

The next morning was a day off, and I was still in my bunk, hung over, when one of the watches woke me up around zero nine hundred hours. Tours for the American community were scheduled that morning, and the Captain had requested that I conduct some of them. After all, I had mentioned how much I enjoyed showing the ship off to our own people, and I had made the statement to the CO. He picked today to make my dream come true. What could I do? I got dressed and had a quick Alka-Seltzer Plus and a few aspirins. I conducted two tours that day. Then I think I took a nap (ah, relief).

Not all the efforts to show the ship turned out to be difficult. The Captain arranged for *Yorktown* to visit Kennebunkport, Maine, and the home of then Vice President George H. W. Bush. That was a great trip. The Veep and his wife, Barbara, were some of the nicest people you could ever meet. They were aboard for a dinner one night and then hosted a cookout for the crew the next day. A photographer with them constantly took pictures. At one point during the dinner aboard ship I asked Mrs. Bush if my friends and I could take a picture with her. She graciously said yes and pulled us all together for the shot. It came out great, and I still have it hanging in my home office.

Vice-President George H. W. Bush on USS *Yorktown (CG-48)* during visit to Kennebunkport, Maine.

After the picture was taken, we thanked her, and as we were moving off, she asked us "Have you guys tried the meatballs? They are very good."

I answered that we had not and was surprised by her reaction. She immediately got a concerned look on her face.

"Did they tell you boys not to eat?" She sounded upset, and I knew that she would take care of the situation if I had said that we were told not to eat. The CO was not that kind of officer, however. So I answered her.

"No, ma'am, they didn't. We can eat anything on the table."

With an even voice she smiled and said, "Well, then go try the meatballs."

We thanked her for the picture again and made an obvious show of going to the meatballs, under her gaze. We each found and slipped into our mouths a delicious meatball. Barbara Bush was very nice and friendly, and meeting her will always be a highlight of my military career.

The gracious Barbara Bush posing with a few giddy sailors. Well, I was, at least. Taken just before she mentioned the meatballs. She was right; they were good.

The vice president had visited the ship for a tour earlier that day. I was assigned outside of Main Engineroom Two (MER2) to welcome him to that space. The Secret Service made at least three walk-throughs on the route around the ship before he did. Later, at the dinner in the hangar, I asked one of them if they had done anything special for his visit to the ship.

"Where could he be safer than aboard a US Navy ship?"

"Did you do a check on the entire crew?" I asked.

"No need to, you are all US sailors, right? Who is there to worry about?"

"Well, no one that will be up here tonight. But to be sure there are a couple of crewmen that are probably below being kept busy so they can't come up here to the reception," I replied.

When he got to MER2, the Veep stopped to talk with me, and I noticed how tall he was and how blue his eyes were. He asked a couple of questions and listened when I answered. I felt that I genuinely had the attention of the Vice President of the United States; he was not just faking it. I saw him next in the Chiefs' Mess where he was reading some of the charge books of our Chief Selectees. If you think having an officer sign your book was a no-no, just think about having the Veep of the nation sign it. George H. W. Bush signed each book and laughed out loud when he read some of what was written in them. He actually repeated word for word and used the exact language that some people had written. It was a good thing a microphone was not around.

The evening dinner aboard the ship was cut short for Mr. and Mrs. Bush due to the death of a friend and Reagan cabinet member. Commerce Secretary Malcolm Baldrige died from injuries suffered in a rodeo accident. He had been riding in a calf-roping event in Brentwood, California.

Entertainer Jimmy Dean was also a guest for the ship's dinner. He struck up a conversation with me on the boat ride out to the ship earlier in the day. "Brother Bishop, how are you?" we were wearing white uniforms and our name badges were on them.

"I'm doing fine, sir. How are you? You're Jimmy Dean, right?" I said.

"Yep. I'm Jimmy Dean, the pork sausage king. You can shake my hand, but you can't beat my meat!" At this his wife looked a little uncomfortable. She probably put up with him the way my wife puts up with me. We talked a bit and then got to the ship and went our different ways.

Later, he requested a tour of the engineering spaces and asked the Captain if "Brother Bishop" could do it. So, we went on a tour. I was showing the ship off to another American. Jimmy Dean has since passed away, but he was around a long time. I remember watching him on television as a kid. When our tour took us into Central Control Station (CCS) I introduced him to the petty officer on watch.

"This is Jimmy Dean," I said, and I waited for a reply. The PO had a blank look on his face.

"'Big Bad John'?" I was referring to the song that Mr. Dean had made so famous in my younger days.

"*The Jimmy Dean Show*?" Still that blank look. "*Diamonds Are Forever*"? I was sure he had seen the James Bond movie Jimmy had been in.

"Jimmy Dean Pork Sausage? He's the king!" The watch was still not impressed.

About that time Jimmy said, "Brother Bishop, don't worry about it; he's too young to remember me."

The Pork Sausage King and I continued on our tour, and I enjoyed the entire time. Before he left he invited me and another crewman to visit his yacht, *Big Bad John*, if we were ever in Fort Lauderdale, Florida. We were there a few months later but did not take him up on the offer.

Chapter 19

"Hey, Bishop's got mail!"

As corny as it may sound, I believe I married the best woman in the world for a man in my chosen occupation. Being the wife of someone who has decided to make a career in the military is not easy. One of the lessons I learned after my retirement was that if a hurricane is screaming toward your home and family it can get scary. It is especially discomforting if you do not have a ship to ride out of harm's way on. During my navy days we had to take the ship to sea away from the hurricane and to a safe place in the Atlantic. Save the ship at all costs. The crew was recalled from liberty, and the ship left port. After I retired I was forced to stay and help with the house and family. That turned hurricanes into a whole different animal to me.

Taking the ships to sea during storms meant that a lot of navy spouses were left alone to hold down the home front. I suppose it is not quite as bad for those spouses who have a husband already out of the country, because they have been gone. To have a husband in port and home most nights and there when they need help but suddenly pulled to the ship and gone in the face of a major storm front has got to be an uncomfortable feeling. It happens to most navy spouses. The storm might not be the worst of it.

When a sailor is on a cruise, the day-to-day operations of the household are the responsibility of the significant other. Everything the kids need, such as medical exams, shoes, school supplies, food, sports, the whole ball of wax, and more. It is all on the spouse's shoulders. Spouses must face every crisis on their own. I have the

128

utmost respect for anyone who can be an effective military mate. Marriage vows should state "through good times and bad times, through richer or poorer, and through military life or until death do you part." The bad times are when she is left for six to nine months to handle every crisis that presents itself. Many women cannot do that. Many marriages are short-lived because of the stress that military life can place upon them.

In the military today the amount of time it takes information to get home and back is as little as a few minutes. The Internet has revolutionized communications between the deployed and the spouse at home. If little Johnny falls out of bed and bangs his head, Daddy knows about it before breakfast, no matter where he is. It is the same with any home-front crisis. When Susie was born, her dad got to see her within moments. Many times he watches the birth via cameras in the delivery room and flat screens at his duty station. It is a vast improvement over the sometimes antiquated communications equipment in my day.

We had to use snail mail, or, actually, super slow snail mail. If the car broke down, it could take over a month for the system to get a letter to the husband at sea. We were used to the lack of mail on a regular basis, but that does not mean we liked it. I learned of my grandmother's death a month after the event. It would have been much faster if someone had thought of the Red Cross for notification, but no one did. They send out a message to the command informing the sailor of the familial death. So we definitely did not like it, but it was all we knew.

Actually, some sailors did like it. They were dreading mail call because they knew that every letter from home brought bad news. The wife complained ceaselessly and blamed his active duty for all of the problems. Some guys got absolutely no support from home. Some got letters saying that they were packing up the kids and going home to Mama's house. The wives of other sailors threatened to divorce and take everything they owned. In the worst-case scenario, the letters from home just simply stopped. That last one can be debilitating to a sailor. There are also those who come home to a house with no furniture and no one living there. If they are lucky, there will be a lawyer with divorce papers waiting for them. At least then they will know what is happening.

Even when the letters continue, they might be few and far between, short on details and long on concepts. The sailor finds out that the barn burned when the tractor crashed into it, but it is a blessing because junior was driving it, and by the way the repair bills are enormous. On the ship he might be asking himself, "So, is junior okay?" Long-distance damage control of your marriage is fate's joke on the human race.

A lot of wives vent their own frustrations in the letter to the husband. They say things like, "This wouldn't happen if you were home; if you do not get out of the service I'll leave you. The kids think their daddy's dead." The sailors read these letters, and there is nothing they can do from a foreign country. They write back, but that is going to take weeks too. After a while depression sets in and usually affects their work. Some start to spiral down in depression, and it is hard to pull them out if it. They avoid mail call as much as possible because they know what is waiting for them. The advent of the Internet hopefully has resolved many of the communications problems we had during my time in the service.

I was lucky. My wife wrote almost every day. Each letter was numbered on the outside so I could read them in order. The cool part is that she started putting perfume on the envelopes, so I could have a reminder of what awaited me at home. She put enough on the letter so that the aroma would last long enough to get to me. So, when the mail bags came aboard, everyone could smell my letters. Even before I got my mail I could hear guys in the passageway, "Hey, Bishop's got mail!" I thought about charging ten cents for the opportunity to sniff my letters but decided against it. Hey, they were mine and mine alone.

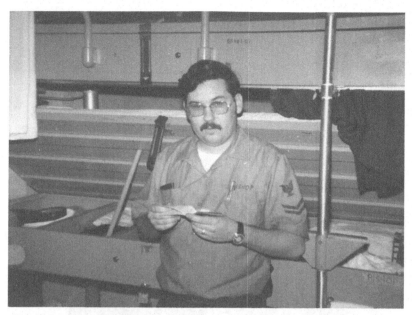

Reading my mail during an earlier part of my career. This was onboard
LaSalle, and I was still a PO2. Taken early 1976.

She never kept things from me when I was deployed, and she
never blamed any problems all on me. She was very self-reliant, and
if it needed to be done she did it. When she could not understand
something, she investigated and found the answers. That was before
the Internet. She wrote two- and three-page letters to me most of
the time. I never got bored with them. As much as some guys used
to disappear at mail call, I made sure I was there.

Homecomings were bittersweet for some crewmen. As the ship
came alongside the pier those of us manning the rail tried to spot
our families. My wife and oldest son were always there waving flags.
I always knew that I would be welcomed with open arms.

My son Seth and my wife Donna waving welcome home flag on the pier.
I always knew they would be there.

Some guys saw that their families were not there, and some saw lawyers, those men on the pier in a snappy suit and a briefcase, waiting for them with divorce papers in hand. I have even witnessed a guy who was met by his wife and kids who were standing not too far from his girlfriend. She was from Europe and had followed him around the Mediterranean Sea, which must have cost a lot of money. I can just imagine how surprised he was to see her in Norfolk, Virginia. He spent a good deal of time trying to find someone whose duty he could take so he did not have to leave the ship. He eventually saw divorce papers too.

As soon as we were secured to the pier and the gangways were in place, the dependents were allowed to climb up the ladder and stream onto the ship. The next couple of hours were chaos aboard as sailors and families tried to find each other in the jammed-packed passageways and messdecks. As the men completed their duties and could leave for home, the bedlam started to die down. Many crewmen put their families on the messdecks while they returned to work putting the ship to bed. There were wives and children onboard for quite a while.

When we had secured the ship and the in-port duty section took over, we went home. I could not wait until I could be home and get what I had wanted for the entire cruise. If your mind is in the gutter right now, you are wrong. Sex is not the first thing I wanted. Believe it or not, I wanted to feel thick, plush carpet under my bare feet. The ship has nothing but hard steel decks to walk on. After months at sea I wanted to take off my shoes and feel the carpet. However, doing this act was a first step in getting undressed and putting me on track to the next thing I wanted after I got home. You can now go to the gutter. After that I wanted a cold beer or two. Once I recovered from the carpet, sex, and beer, it was repeat each step as necessary.

My wife's support from across the sea included periodically sending me care packages. Now, do not get me wrong. There were many wives of the officers and crew who sent supportive mail and care packages; my wife was not the only one. But she is the one I speak of. Some of the care packages included everything from cookies to books, toys, and VHS tapes of new television shows. The new technology in today's navy is the Internet and the ease of communication between the deployed ship and the crew's family. The last time I went on deployment the big thing was the VCR in the mess. We could watch what we wanted and when we wanted it. That was a nice step in our day.

During meals and in the evenings, the Chiefs' Mess televisions were running constantly. Everyone had different schedules, so there was a need to replay the tapes enough times for everyone to see the shows on it. If the tape had something exceptional it was kept, while we returned the regular shows to the wife who had sent it, to record on and mail back to us. It was a newly received tape from my wife that became known as the "*Night Court* Incident," at least to me. It ruined my lunch for sure and almost ruined my career too.

The television series *Night Court* was very popular at the time, and it was the same onboard the *Yorktown*. It was always a treat when a new tape arrived and included that show on it. The first lunch after we got it was crowded, because every chief wanted to see the show as soon as possible. I happened to be eating lunch on time once, a rare occurrence, and a tape sent by my wife was up to be watched that day. Someone just popped the tape into the machine, and it picked up where it had left off the previous showing. *Night Court* started to play.

The plot of the episode I am speaking of now was something to do with breast size. The cast included Marky Post, an attractive blonde woman who most of the guys lusted after when they saw her on the small screen. Throughout the story breast size was discussed, and her size was a major question. The men were always trying to find out for sure what size they were. Basically there was a constant tease about breasts. We watched it to the finale. At that point Ms. Post jumps up, grabs the front of her shirt, and rips it open, showing her breasts. This was a very interesting part of the show. Unfortunately, right at that moment the tape stopped. Right as the program would have shown her front view, the show disappeared from the screen. Everybody knows that nothing would actually have been shown, but it was the thought that counts. It got extremely quiet in the chiefs' mess, which was unnatural, at best. All eyes turn to me in an accusing fashion. The crowd started to get ugly. Then we found out what had happened. The tape was at the end. It had simply run out at that particular moment. Donna had no idea it had done that because she always put it on timed record. When it was finished recording, she put it back in the sleeve it came in and dropped it into the box for mailing.

"Hey, what happened? You're dead, Bishop!" someone in the mob yelled. "She did that on purpose," cried another. I heard, "Stone the bum, hangin's too good for 'em!"

My lunch was over. I was being harassed too much to continue. I am glad that they did not have rotten tomatoes at their disposal. I was already getting pelted with stuff. I was safer in the engineering spaces, where I could do something useful. I do not believe my fellow chiefs ever forgave me for that, and I do not know about them, but to this day I have never seen the end of that episode. My *Night Court* incident will live with me forever. The thought of that day still makes me laugh.

Chapter 20

"Those Chiefs are going to kill me . . ."

When the ship was in homeport a liberal leave policy was usually in effect. This was particularly the case after a major deployment. Engineering was almost always in three section duty, even when the plant was secured, and we were in a cold iron status. Cold iron meant that most of the plant was secured or turned off, and we were receiving shore power, water, and sewage, among other things, from pier services. Every third day I was aboard with the duty section monitoring the machinery spaces and equipment.

Usually on duty days in homeport things were quiet after working hours. Weekends were quiet too. On Saturdays and Sundays my wife and oldest son came aboard for lunch or dinner or just to visit. If there were no mechanical casualties, I could spend a fair amount of time with them.

One day my son, who was only six or seven years old, said that he wanted to see more of the ship. I was proud that my son wanted to see the ship I worked on, and he was showing interest in my profession. The tour went well, and I showed him the engineering spaces; he was not too impressed with those. He was more interested in the berthing areas, messdecks, and the bridge. He also liked seeing the weapons, and missile and gun mounts. After a while we were back in the Chiefs' Mess. I understood that it was probably not the exciting military installations that he saw in movies and television.

But he really knocked the wind out of my proud daddy sails when he said, "But, Dad, where are the real army guys?"

During some of their visits on the weekends my family had to spend time alone if there were problems in the spaces. As the Engineering Officer of the Watch (EOOW), I had to respond to machinery causalities such as pumps breaking down, electric motors burning out, and more, to at least find out what was wrong. Ship readiness was the most important overriding factor in everything we did. Many times I just had to develop status reports while the men assigned to do the job worked their magic. I remember the troops saying under their breaths, "There's Senior Chief Bishop; pick up the tools, quick," whenever I entered the work area to help. Like me when I was in that position, they did not want the Senior Chief using any tools and gumming up the works. Of course, in my case, they were joking . . . I think.

On one of the days when the family visited I had to leave to help with a mechanical problem. They were left alone in the mess to cool their heels, and my wife got bored. She was feeling industrious that day. The mess looked as though it had been lived in for a while without a proper cleaning. So, my lovely wife set about straightening up the kitchen area and the lounge area. She put all the cushions in their right spots. Things were picked up off the floor; she may have even vacuumed the floor. The tables got a good cleaning and dishes were put in the sink and coffee cups were returned to the board for cups by the coffee urn. I was away for some time, and she was still in the cleaning mode.

When I arrived back in the mess, she was still cleaning. I was stunned when I saw what her cleaning targets were. She had started cleaning the coffee cups that the chiefs used personally. Sailors never wash their coffee cups. They just rinse them out, leaving each cup with a stain of coffee inside. Over the course of years using the same cup, that patina builds layer on top of layer until the inside of the cup is black. Most sailors are extremely proud of the buildup in their cups. After all, it shows how long they have been drinking coffee in the navy and how strong they like their coffee. As grody as the cups get, the owner keeps building it up.

I saw what she was doing, and I think I let out a scream. It might even have been a girlie scream. I noticed that there were only about three cups already cleaned. I had gotten there in time to save most of them. I stared at the newly cleaned cups and said, "Those chiefs are going to kill me . . ."

"Why? Did you see how dirty they were?"

"Babe, sit down. I've got to explain something to you." I told her what a sin she had just committed. She could still not understand the attraction of having a filthy-looking coffee cup. I do not believe she comprehends the tradition even today. She never tried to clean the Chiefs' Mess again.

She mumbled, "If they don't appreciate it, they can clean it themselves."

She still continued to visit but never touched the coffee cup board again. The Chiefs whose cups were cleaned never let me hear the end of it.

I never heard the end of the "*Night Court* Incident" either. Every time someone put a VHS tape into the player, they would look around, and if I was in the space they would ask out loud, "Hey, this isn't one of Bishop's tapes, is it?" Then everybody had to chuckle or snicker or make some other gross sounds. See the chapter titled "Hey, Bishop's got mail." for an explanation of the *Night Court* reference.

Chapter 21

"Now there's an odd duck, if I've ever seen one."

Finally, there are people I have met and things I have seen that bear mentioning. Maybe these items do not rate an entire chapter, page, or even a whole paragraph, but I feel that they do indeed require a call out. In this chapter I will be citing some of those in no particular order.

You have not lived until you have sat in the Chiefs' Mess with fifteen to twenty chiefs off a German Navy ship watching the movie *The Dirty Dozen*. They were cheering both sides of the conflict. Whenever anyone got shot for any reason, they got a hell of a charge out of it. The American chiefs kept the cheering to a minimum. We were too cool. They were visiting because both ships were in the same port and hosting each other. They invited our Chiefs' Mess to their floating abode, and we took them up on it.

No movie in their mess, but they did have alcohol, so we made do. It was hard but, after all, we needed to be polite, right? They were a bunch of nice guys, and I think all the chiefs from both messes had a good time. A sad note here; a few weeks later we heard that their ship had had a fire at sea, and I think there were causalities. But, do not quote me on that.

Sleeping soundly onboard a navy ship is not always possible. Because watch teams change every four hours, guys are coming and going all night long. Most try to be quiet, but there are some who could not care less and let their bunk lockers slam shut loudly or otherwise make noise. When a member of the off-going section enters the berthing compartment to wake up reliefs, he is not always prepared with lists on where each relief sleeps. This causes a guessing game to start while they find people, going from rack to rack knocking and moving curtains to determine who to wake. All this causes a commotion that wakes up a lot of guys.

Because you are disturbed a couple of times each night you get to see a lot of the rituals performed in the dark by those getting up for watch. I remember when I was in the E-6 and below berthing that one of the Third Class Petty Officers had a strange habit of smelling his socks before he put them on. I first assumed that he had placed a clean pair of socks in his shoes before he went to sleep so they would be ready when he got up. Through the use of observation and deduction I realized that he smelled the dirty socks from the day prior. He then put them on.

He had a certain ritual he followed each time. Once he was awake he would get dressed with the exception of footwear and sit on the deck between the racks in a crossed-leg Indian style. He followed that by pulling the dirty sock from one shoe and stretching it out with his hands. He would then start at the toe of the sock and sniff until he got to the heel. After he was satisfied, for whatever reason, he put the sock on and started with the other shoe. Science tells us that smells, aromas, and pheromones can be very arousing to humans. I cannot imagine what dirty socks from an old set of boondockers could arouse. I never asked him, either.

Later, another petty officer asked me if I had noticed the midnight sock smelling. I acknowledged that I had and thought it was pretty strange. We talked about people and their quirks a few minutes.

Then, in reference to our sock lover, I said, "Now there's an odd duck, if I've ever seen one." I was to see many odd ducks in my navy career, and they never ceased to amaze me.

Once in a while something catches you so totally off guard that you are left dumbstruck. That is what happened to me in Hamburg, Germany. The ship had pulled into Kiel, Germany, for a visit and to "show the flag," as we always did in foreign ports. After the up and over lights were rigged and shore services taken care of, we were ready for liberty call. The first stop after leaving the ship was the first bar we came to. We had a couple of cold ones, and someone suggested that we catch a train to Hamburg. I did enjoy Germany. We were there a few days, and the time off was great. But with all the fun we had while there, I can still only really remember one incident that got to me. We were at a large intersection in Hamburg waiting to cross. There seemed to be hundreds of cars and thousands of people all going in different directions. It was a little confusing.

I was looking around at all the sights, and my eyes happened to drop to the little girl standing next to me. She looked up at me too. It hit me just how pretty she was—that Nordic look of bright blue eyes and light blonde hair along with the smoothest skin you can imagine. I swear that I was instantly in love with a ten-year-old. She was just so pretty. Being the guy that I am, I could not resist saying hello. So I looked down and said "hi" while I waved my hand at her.

The angelic expression on her face disappeared and a look of pure evil (can you say Damien, anyone) contorted her features. She raised a hand with the middle finger extended to her lips and kissed the tip of the finger. Then, while she raised her hand farther up into my face, she pursed her lips and made a shrill whistling sound as she flipped me off. I have to tell you, I was more than a little stunned. The light changed, and the world went on rotating. I just stood there watching the evil princess walk away.

I could not believe it. What the hell was her problem? The next time I saw a mirror I double-checked to see if I had "American sailor" written on my face. I did not.

On the USS *Spruance* I visited quite a few countries and enjoyed all of them, though some more than others. One visit was to Monrovia, Liberia, in West Africa. As you would expect, it is a very poor country. The city of Monrovia was named after American President James Monroe, who was a staunch advocate of resettling American slaves on the African continent. When we were there I felt that they were still very pro-America. When liberty call sounded we went ashore as usual. However, because it was some type of holiday or something, we had to wear our white uniforms. I remember that it was very hot and very dusty and very noisy. We had hit the trifecta!

Catching a cab from fleet landing to the city proper was a trip. The ride was very fast and plenty dusty. By the time it was over you would have needed a beer if you did not already need one. The ride was a little longer then it had to be because the taxi driver wanted to show us his home. When we swung by his place, it was really a shack built from discarded wooden pallets. He was most proud of his new front door.

The abode was very small and had to be cramped, but it had a new front door made from a big red Coca-Cola sign standing on the edge. It looked like a new sign had been ripped from its place and brought here. Standing like it was, it probably measured four feet wide by six feet tall. I have to admit that in comparison to the dwellings around him, the taxi driver's house looked good with the shiny new red sign.

As in most foreign ports, there were the obligatory "Hey-Joes." Those are the small street urchins who constantly beg and bother you for everything from gum and chocolate to cold hard cash. It is a way for them to meet Americans and get money to help them survive. Again, as in most foreign ports, we found the nearest bar. Inside the bar it was not quite as hot as it was outside, and before long a lot of the ship's company turned up in that establishment. The beer was only passable, but it was the only beer in town. That meant every cantina in the city had the same brand of beer. Whatever is in the ingredients of that brew, it gave us all humongous headaches pretty fast. But after you have had a few beers the aches disappeared, at least until the next morning.

The Joes had stayed outside in the blinding sun. I think that the bartender kept them out so we could drink and spend our money in peace. But an older fellow did sneak in to harass us. He did not look like your typical Hey-Joe, so the bartender had not noticed him. Of course, the bartender could have been splitting the profits with him, who knows? He did have a novel approach, however. I was sitting by the door, and he came to me first. He got my attention and said to me, "For five dollars I'll leave you alone." His English surprised me.

I asked, "*What?*" He gave me a snaggletooth smile.

He repeated his offer. Here was a Hey-Joe with style. While the others scrambled up and down your back yelling for money, he simply got straight to the point. He wanted money, and we wanted to be left alone. It was a good business proposal. He probably had an MBA from the Liberian University of Hey-Joes. But I was not buying.

"See that tall guy over by the bar?" I asked and pointed to our Master Chief. "You'd have better luck with him." Joe moved off in that direction to offer his deal.

Now the Master Chief, I'll just use Kay for his last name, is tall and lanky, and he does not suffer fools easily. I think he had been a police officer in Columbus, Ohio, but found that it was more dangerous than defending the country so he returned to the navy. He was a great guy and had a good sense of humor. I do not think he was buying either. That is why I sent the burgeoning businessman over to him.

I turned and watched as he went up to the Master Chief. I could not hear what they said to each other, but I could clearly see that he was making the same offer. Master rolled his cigar around in his mouth as though he were in deep thought. He put his hand on his hip and leaned down to the guy's face and said something. I could not hear this one-way exchange either, but whatever the Master Chief said sent this guy scurrying out the door and into the sun. For his part, the Master Chief rolled his stogie again (deep in thought?), glanced at our table (at me?), and went back to his beer.

I do not remember if the Master Chief ever said anything to me about the Hey-Joe in Monrovia or not, and I do not know what he said that sent the guy out the door. What I do know is that Master Chief definitely had a sense of humor. Not long after checking aboard USS *Spruance* my wife was dropping me off for work in front of the pier. Master Chief was coming from the CPO parking lot (yeah, they get their own parking lot) and was walking right toward us.

When he got to us I said, "Master Chief, I'd like you to meet my wife, Donna." Then, looking down at her, I continued, "Donna, this is Master Chief Kay."

She said, "Hi."

He said, "Right, yeah, well, it's nice to meet you, Donna."

Well, that went okay, I thought. But before she could pull away, Master Chief looked at her, shook his head, and looked at me and said, "Hey, Bishop, she's nowhere near as fat as you said she was."

"Oh, yeah, right!" I said, thinking to myself, "Master Chief, what a funny fuckin' dude."

She drove off, and we headed for the ship.

Another run-in with the shore patrol happened in the streets of Jacksonville, Florida (Jax). We had tied up at Naval Station Mayport, just east of Jax. A group of us went to St. Augustine to see the Spanish fort and other sights. We rode a bus from Mayport to Jacksonville and then on to St. Augustine. It was still early in what would turn out to be a long day. Our first clue of how the day would go was in the bus terminal restaurant waiting for the bus to St. Augustine. We had already seen more shore patrol presence than we would normally expect. Two of them came into the Jax bus terminal and came directly to us. We had been sitting there sipping our cokes and shooting the breeze when they came up. They told us to show them our ID cards. One of my shipmates fancied himself a sea lawyer and said, "You can't hassle us. We ain't done anything wrong."

The look on their faces told me right away that they could hassle us, and it was now their intention to do so. We all showed them our navy ID cards, and they found nothing wrong, so they left, moving on to the next table. Luckily the shipmate who opened his mouth saw fit to keep it shut the rest of the time they were with us. We caught the bus and visited St. Augustine and had a good time.

On the way back to the ship we again had to wait in the Jacksonville terminal. No shore patrol was evident this time because they were out on the streets keeping drunken sailors under control. The sun had set, and we decided to hit a couple of entertainment establishments with all the other sailors who were having fun. We would catch a later bus to the base. Long story short, we got pretty into the bag that night. I mean we were drunk! I do not know if I was older than the drinking age or not. I do know that we were all tired and just wanted to get back to our racks. Of course, we were now drunk on our asses and probably not making much sense to those who are sober. Rather than wait for the bus to take us back, one of the guys had a great idea. His plan was simple, as he demonstrated. He walked over to the shore patrol paddy wagon and asked if they could give him a ride back to the base. The big one said, "Sure."

Both of them opened the wagon's back door, put handcuffs on my friend, and threw him into the wagon. "Anyone else want a ride?" There were no takers.

We had hung back to keep them from smelling booze on our breath. The sea lawyer in our group picked this moment to practice law. "Hey!" he yelled at our shipmate, who was now in the back of the paddy wagon, "They can't do that to you!"

One of the SPs had been leaning into the back of the van fiddling with something as though he was securing his prisoner. He pulled his head back out of the wagon and looked directly at the idiot who had just said that. "You want a ride too?" Again, there were no takers.

Alcohol was an occupational hazard when I joined the navy. It was an expected part of everyday life. We were young and dumb and full of piss and vinegar. Some of you thought I was going to say something other than piss and vinegar, right? Anyway, every night was party night. And those who did not have duty staggered back to the ship at all hours of the night. That was all well and good unless you lived and slept on the ship or were part of the duty section.

The most obnoxious people in the world are the drunks coming into the berthing area in the middle of the night. They have no concept of quiet. Some are so drunk that they cannot find the head to take that last leak before going to bed. More than a couple of times I know of incidences where a guy peed right there between the racks, thinking in his drunken haze that he was in the head standing before a urinal. Unfortunately, some were actually peeing on the bunk below them. That would be bad enough if the bunk was not your own, but if the owner was also a current occupant, it could be dangerous.

A number of guys have awakened to find themselves being peed on by a wiped-out shipmate. Again, that is extremely dangerous, and many sailors do not wake up in a good mood. They are twice as grumpy when they are being peed on. The pounding they give is to ensure that the drunk who pissed in their racks never does it again. It contributes to an even worse headache the next day because of it.

As I reflect upon those crazy times and some of the big mistakes I made or the times I have made an ass of myself, I can pretty much blame my drinking for the rough times. Like many people, I made better decisions when sober than I did when drunk. It has been over twenty years since I have had a drink of alcohol, and I have not missed it a bit. I highly recommend sobriety for everyone. If I have learned one thing in my life it is that life is much better when you are sober.

Cigarette smokers are a different lot. They can come back drunk and find the head in most cases, from my experience. The problem they have, and it is one that will turn an easy-going Rich Bishop into a violent individual, is lighting up in their bunks. It is unnerving to me to wake up smelling smoldering blankets and mattresses. I would rather smell my socks. Before I moved into the chiefs' berthing, I personally dragged two fellow sailors from their racks. When I say drag, I mean I pulled them, mattress and all, out and onto the floor. Fire aboard ship is not a pleasant thing to behold. Everyone knew the dangers of smoking in your rack. You can beat my sister, but do not set my berthing area on fire.

Mustering the Engineering Department on *Yorktown*. This represents just a few of the great shipmates I served with during my career. Some of these guys are young and hold a lot of responsibility. The nation's security depends upon young men and women just like these. You can hate their mission, but love those sailors.

Tobacco chewers are another case altogether. Aside from always trying to talk guys out of chewing for their health, the fact that most of them have no consideration for people around them makes me want to somehow put an end to the nasty habit for good. Now, most of them will tell you that they are not the problem. It is always the others who chew that make the messes, spill their cans, and spit into someone else's soda can, and on and on. But, if you watch carefully you will see that every chewer is sloppy. If you are around them with a soda can, be sure to keep an eye on it so they do not spit into your soda can by accident. I have never had it happen to me, but I have seen other guys take a drink and get spit instead of what they were expecting. *That* does not make for happy campers. If the drinker coldcocks the chewer, I guess that is just between them. I am not going to say anything.

Chapter 22

"You won't have Dick Bishop to kick around anymore!"

As I look back I sometimes wonder at my luck in relation to my navy career. In my memories I can see people who helped me zig when I should have zigged and zag when I should have zagged. They helped me color within the lines. I met a lot of good men and women. I enjoyed camaraderie with shipmates that you have to experience to understand. When I started my civilian career I enjoyed the places where I worked and had no problems with the people working beside me. But there was always something missing. I can only feel that the missing element was the military cohesiveness born of serving your country together in far-off lands. Almost sounds poetic, doesn't it?

Memories are great and nice to relive. But the true test, and answers, of how well I served the US Navy comes when you take into consideration a few facts. I joined in the 1960s, so I was part of the so-called "Old Navy" that so many of my shipmates longed to return to. Old Navy was anything prior to 1970. I also helped train the "New Navy" during my career. That there was a difference between old and new speaks to the need for successful progression from one to the other. You can say I helped bring the US Navy into the future.

As I served, the force achieved a fleet in excess of six hundred ships. My presence did not prevent that from happening. People I served with were routinely promoted through the ranks. Knowing me did not retard their mobility. When I retired in 1992 the US

Navy was as strong as or stronger than ever before. After all these years since I left active duty, the navy seems to be steaming right along no worse for the wear.

Crew habitability has improved immensely since those olden days of the 1960s. So, I left the navy with more, newer ships, better-trained personnel, and cleaner living conditions for the crew, and I left them in good enough shape when I retired that the navy is still running without my guiding hand. All that being said, I guess I must've been a positive influence on the organization as a whole.

I have always been a history nut as far as trivia goes. I do not remember many big dates, but those smaller dates stick to me like albatrosses coming into my mind when I least expect them. I usually have ridiculously unimportant information for all to hear. Not that many listen, however. I also like to use quotes from famous and infamous historical personalities. If you are quick enough you can fit an interesting quote into any conversation. Because we have the same first name I am particularly fond of a certain Richard M. Nixon quote.

After being vice president of the United States for eight years, Nixon ran for president against the Democratic candidate John F. Kennedy in 1960. Anyone who remembers Mr. Nixon can attest that he and the news media had a rocky, at best, relationship. The election was very close, but Kennedy was declared the winner. Nixon looked for reasons to explain why he had lost so close a race. His reasons went from the newspeople not covering his campaign properly, his being sick during the televised debate, to even the media purposely acting against his success. After the Inaugural of JFK, Nixon returned to his home in California.

Soon he was running for governor of California in 1962 against Pat Brown. Once again he lost the big one. With even more blame given to the news media, he decided to quit politics and practice law. At a press conference where he made the announcement he got in what he thought would be his final dig at the media when he said, "You won't have Nixon to kick around anymore . . ." I always add the first name in the quote when I use it. It is better when you are leaving a big event. You can quote the line and make a grand

149

exit. Every time I transferred I used it to signal that I was gone for good.

This has been a real pleasure for me to write a little about my navy career. In a way, it has been a cathartic endeavor. Writing about some of this stuff has given me a new perspective on past events. I can now see them for what they were . . . just random events in my life. I realize that there is probably another volume in my head. Hey, maybe two more. I think there would be enough to keep it clean too. In twenty-two years, five months, and twenty-four days, I think that there is more to reveal. When this one hits the best-seller list I will start part two.

I highly recommend that everybody try their hand at writing their life story. It is a shame that most books cover the wardroom and its denizens. The enlisted side needs to be told more often. Whether or not I actually come up with a second volume, this one is over for now, and I will leave you with a good-bye. Just know that from now until then, "You won't have Dick Bishop to kick around anymore!"

January 1992. My last moments in uniform. After the retirement
ceremony I went home and posed for this picture and changed into
civilian clothes. It had been approximately twenty-two years, five
months, twenty-four days, and ten hours, give or take depending upon
the coast you are on, since I donned my first uniform. Too bad those
marines that met the bus in November 1969 could not see me now.

My favorite verse from the "Navy Hymn"

"Eternal Father, Strong to save,
Whose arm hath bound the restless wave,
Who bid'st the mighty Ocean deep
Its own appointed limits keep;
O hear us when we cry to thee,
for those in peril on the sea."
Rev. William Whiting (1825–78)